After Corporate Paternalism

After Corporate Paternalism

Material Renovation and Social Change in Times of Ruination

Christian Straube

berghahn
NEW YORK · OXFORD
www.berghahnbooks.com

First published in 2021 by
Berghahn Books
www.berghahnbooks.com

© 2021, 2023 Christian Straube
First paperback edition published in 2023

Library of Congress Cataloging-in-Publication Data
A C.I.P. cataloging record is available from the Library of Congress
Library of Congress Cataloging in Publication Control Number: 2021015487

British Library Cataloguing in Publication Data
A catalogue record for this book is available from the British Library

ISBN 978-1-80073-133-2 hardback
ISBN 978-1-80073-932-1 paperback
ISBN 978-1-80073-415-9 open access ebook

https://doi.org/10.3167/9781800731332

An electronic version of this book is freely available thanks to the support of
libraries working with Knowledge Unlatched. KU is a collaborative initiative
designed to make high-quality books Open Access for the public good. More
information about the initiative and links to the Open Access version can be
found at knowledgeunlatched.org.

To the people of Mpatamatu

Contents

List of Illustrations   viii

Acknowledgements   x

List of Abbreviations   xii

Introduction. Things Fall Apart   1

Chapter 1. Of Company and Government   19

Chapter 2. Of Men and Women   48

Chapter 3. Of Miners and Teachers   68

Chapter 4. Of Miners and Preachers   87

Conclusion. Things Reassembled   115

References   123

Index   144

Illustrations

Maps

0.1. Mpatamatu township. OpenStreetMaps with data collected by
the author.   xvii

0.2. Zambia's Copperbelt with its most important towns and mines
on both sides of its border with the Democratic Republic of
the Congo (DRC). Jutta Turner (Max Planck Institute for Social
Anthropology, Halle/Saale).   8

1.1. Luanshya with its European and African mine and municipal
townships, 1951. LSE Library Archives, London.   28

1.2. Mpatamatu's planned section 21, 1957. ZCCM-IH Archives,
Ndola.   31

Figures

0.1. The signposts and metal arch welcoming the visitor to Luanshya.
Photo by the author.   4

0.2. Roan Mpatamatu Mine Township Management Board's
coat of arms. ZCCM-IH Archives, Ndola.   9

0.3. The author's mother in an arts class at Buna's *Haus der
Freundschaft*, 1968. Photo provided by the author's mother.   9

1.1. Mpatamatu's section 22 under construction, late 1950s.
LSE Library Archives, London.   34

1.2. Mpatamatu's section 23, 1964. ZCCM-IH Archives, Ndola.   35

2.1. A 'category 5A' mine house from Mpatamatu's section 23. Photo
by the author.   51

2.2. Former Kabulangeti Community Centre in section 24. Photo by
the author.   58

2.3. Former Muliashi Community Centre in section 26. Photo by
the author.   59

2.4. ZCCM payslip of an underground miner, 1992. Document
courtesy of resident of Mpatamatu.   62

3.1. Classroom of Suzika Private School in section 21's former pay
line buildings. Photo by the author.   77

3.2. Former Kansengu Community Centre in section 21. Photo by
the author.   78

3.3. Mpatamatu College of Education at former Kabulangeti
Community Centre. Photo by the author.   80

4.1. Kansumbi Tavern in section 25. Photo by the author.   91

4.2. Mpatamatu stadium. Photo by the author.   94

4.3. Mpatamatu's former sports complex. Photo by the author.   97

4.4. Former Kabulangeti Tavern in section 23. Photo by the author.   102

4.5. The prayer room in former Kabulangeti Tavern. Photo by
the author.   103

4.6. The main hall of Mpatamatu's former sports complex. Photo by
the author.   105

5.1. The remnants of the entrance to Mpatamatu stadium. Photo by
the author.   120

Tables

0.1. Luanshya as an ethnographic field site.   15

1.1. Mpatamatu's former social welfare buildings.   45

Acknowledgements

This project started in 2012 as an enquiry into China–Africa relations. I would like to thank Professor Joachim Kurtz of Heidelberg University for accompanying me from Chinese revolutionaries in Malaya to Chinese mining companies in Zambia. I also thank Professor Mamadou Diawara and Professor Hans-Peter Hahn of the University of Frankfurt for encouraging me to conduct ethnographic fieldwork and seek a new disciplinary home in social anthropology.

In June 2014, I joined the Max Planck Institute for Social Anthropology in Halle/Saale. I would like to thank Professor Günther Schlee for his unbroken support during the ensuing four years. I also thank Professor Nina Glick Schiller for introducing me to the work of Max Gluckman and the Rhodes-Livingstone Institute; and Professor Robert Home at Anglia Ruskin University for giving me advice on colonial town planning in southern Africa after I returned from fieldwork in October 2016.

At the Max Planck Institute for Social Anthroplogy, I would like to thank Viktoria Giehler-Zeng, Anett Kirchhof, Bettina Mann, Anja Neuner, Kathrin Niehuus, Manuela Pusch, Cornelia Schnepel, Ingrid Schüler, Viola Stanisch and Nadine Wagenbrett for their support before, during and after my fieldwork. Together, they created a unique research environment for me that took account of personal issues related to my family. I also thank the following for their advice on how best to turn my data into a written ethnography: Sandra Calkins, Brian Campbell, James Carrier, Brian Donahoe, John Eidson, Pamila Gupta, Patience Mususa, Tabea Scharrer and Lyn Schumaker.

In July 2015, my family and I arrived in Zambia; I would like to thank Jessica Achberger for giving us such a good start. I also thank the Southern African Institute for Policy and Research, particularly Marja Hinfelaar, for institutional and personal support during our fifteen months in Zambia. Many people helped us settle down and feel at home, including Fröschl and Uta, Lea and Lebo, Mike and the extended Fisher family, Martha, Priscilla, Edna and Joseph, Alison and Matthew, and Ntiusya and Debbie. I also thank Juliet and Felix, Boniface, Samuel, Lilian and Mathews, and Mercy and Humphrey for their support and friendship and for accepting me into their lives.

Our time in Zambia was full of challenges that we would not have been able to overcome without the support of our family and friends. I would like to thank the readers of our private blog who commented on it and accompanied us through internet calls. I thank all those who visited us in Zambia, particularly my parents, parents-in-law, maternal aunt, uncle and cousins, and Katja and Tilman. I would like to thank Erik for virtually following my footsteps in Mpatamatu and turning the GPS data into such a wonderful township map. Thank you, Franz, for being with me since we first landed in Beijing on a September morning thirteen years ago.

I thank my children for keeping me grounded over these past seven years. My last words belong to Nora. We have tried to find our way in Zambia, manoeuvring through all sorts of situations, moments of excitement, disillusion, joy, frustration, encouragement and giving up. Thank you for your love and company!

Abbreviations

15MCC	China 15th Metallurgical Construction Group Corporation
ANC	African National Congress
AIDS	Acquired immune deficiency syndrome
BGRIMM	Beijing General Research Institute of Mining and Metallurgy
BSAC	British South Africa Company
CLM	CNMC Luanshya Copper Mines
CNMC	China Nonferrous Metal Mining (Group) Corporation
CSR	Corporate Social Responsibility
DRC	Democratic Republic of the Congo
DWCI	Dynamic Worship Church International
FQM	First Quantum Minerals
GDR	German Democratic Republic
GPS	Global Positioning System
IMF	International Monetary Fund
KCM	Konkola Copper Mines
LCM	Luanshya Copper Mines
LMC	Luanshya Municipal Council
LME	London Metal Exchange
LSE	London School of Economics and Political Science

MCM	Mopani Copper Mines
MDGi	Millennium Development Goals Initiative
MMD	Movement for Multi-Party Democracy
MMTMB	Mpatamatu Mine Township Management Board
MOFCOM	Ministry of Commerce of the People's Republic of China
MPACE	Mpatamatu College of Education
MUZ	Mineworkers Union of Zambia
NFCA	Non-Ferrous China-Africa
NGO	Non-Governmental Organization
NORTEC	Northern Technical College
PAOC	Pentecostal Assemblies of Canada
PAOG(Z)	Pentecostal Assemblies of God (Zambia)
PF	Patriotic Front
PNT	Privatization Negotiation Team
PRC	People's Republic of China
RACM	Roan Antelope Copper Mines
RAID	Rights and Accountability in Development
RAMCOZ	Roan Antelope Mining Corporation of Zambia
RARC	Roan Antelope Recreation Club
RCM	Roan Consolidated Mines
RLI	Rhodes-Livingstone Institute
RMMTMB	Roan Mpatamatu Mine Township Management Board
RST	Roan Selection Trust
SASAC	State-owned Assets Supervision and Administration Commission of the State Council of the People's Republic of China
SCOAN	The Synagogue, Church of All Nations
UCZ	United Church of Zambia
UMCB	United Missions in the Copper Belt
UMHK	Union Minière du Haut Katanga
UNICEF	United Nations International Children's Emergency Fund
UNIP	United National Independence Party
UPND	United Party for National Development
ZAMEFA	Metal Fabricators of Zambia
ZCCM	Zambia Consolidated Copper Mines

ZCCZ   Zambia–China Economic and Trade Cooperation Zone
ZESCO   Zambia Electricity Supply Corporation
ZNPF   Zambia National Provident Fund

Map 0.1. Mpatamatu township map. OpenStreetMaps with data collected by the author.

Introduction

Things Fall Apart

In his postcolonial classic, *Things Fall Apart*, Chinua Achebe (2001) tells the story of Okonkwo, an Igbo clansman in eastern Nigeria at the turn of the twentieth century. Achebe sketches out a dystopian vision evolving from his lead character's fallibility as a human being during the onset of British colonialism. Okonkwo failed to defend the social order that had initially produced him as a respected member of Igbo society from the Christian mission and colonial government. In the end, Achebe lets Okonkwo commit suicide in an apocalyptic moment reminiscent of W.B. Yeats's poem 'The Second Coming'. Its third line provided the title for Achebe's novel. The reader is left with Okonkwo dead, his world having fallen apart.

I thought about Achebe's novel many times before, during and after my fieldwork in Zambia; in fact, it accompanied me throughout the writing process. When I first read Ferguson's *Expectations of Modernity* (1999), I saw Okonkwo in the mineworkers faced with rural retirement after living for years in the Copperbelt's mining towns. I saw Okonkwo in the Lamba chiefs who had been forced into agreements with the British South Africa Company (BSAC), ceding their rights to the land to industrial exploitation. I saw Okonkwo in the Bemba chiefs confronted with the exodus of men from their villages and the collapse of the rural economy. I saw Okonkwo in the mineworkers who were made redundant and retrenched in the early 2000s after the state-owned copper mining company had been broken up. I saw Okonkwo in the residents of Luanshya's former mine township of Mpatamatu faced with the decaying material remains of four decades of corporate paternalism.

I literally observed how 'things fall apart' in Mpatamatu. This ruinous process expressed itself most prominently in the crumbling infrastructures of the township. There were the run-down mine houses lining the pot-holed streets with broken street lights above them. The rusting headgear of two shafts towered over Mpatamatu. Then there were the township's former social welfare buildings, which became the starting point for my enquiry into people's living conditions. Taverns, clubs, clinics, community centres and sports facilities – everything had been built by the mine, but now they had been left to rot. Mining companies refocused on mines as sites of mineral extraction and abandoned their social facilities. The corporate paternalism of the colonial and post-independence era that had shaped the lives of the mineworkers and their dependants had been replaced by a neoliberal corporate policy characterized by 'millennial capitalism' (Comaroff and Comaroff 2000).

However, I quickly learned that things left behind were reassembled, that is, repaired, reused and reappropriated. Mine clubs were maintained as social centres, a youth centre was turned into a carpenter's shop, a mine clinic became the headquarters of a local non-governmental organization (NGO), and a tavern and the township's sports complex were turned into churches. A local football club continued to use the stadium. Fans cheered from the broken stands, which on other days were used as an auditorium. Former mine houses, now the property of private individuals, were repainted and extended, accommodating car repair shops, grocery stores, barbers, house churches and guest houses. The mine's presence in Mpatamatu had dissolved into numerous individual projects.

Over the decade leading up to my own fieldwork, Stoler (2008b, 2013, 2016: 336–79) had been developing and revisiting the concept of 'ruination' in her academic work on the aftermath of colonialism. Shifting from the material leftovers of 'the ruin', she draws attention to 'ruin' as an active process, to its material and social ramifications. She turns to 'what people are "left with"': to what remains, to the aftershocks of empire, to the material and social afterlife of structures, sensibilities, and things'. To talk of ruins is to focus not on 'inert remains' but on their 'vital refiguration' (Stoler 2008b: 194). Ruins have to be studied as 'epicenters of renewed claims, as history in a spirited voice, as sites that animate new possibilities, bids for entitlement, and unexpected political projects' (Stoler 2008b: 198). It was the temporal and spatial extension from a material site to a socio-material process that caught my interest.

Ruination as a socio-material process rooted in colonial and neoliberal dispossession reverberated with Cane's reading of Mitchell's (2002: 1–2) idea that 'landscape is part of the operation of power' and 'should be considered a verb' (Cane 2019: 3, 173). In Mpatamatu, power operated through the absence of corporate and the inadequacy of municipal 'landscaping'. This gap was filled by private initiative. On a practical ethnographic level, I did not encounter the township's former social welfare buildings as ruins but as sites of creative opportunity. I came to understand their potency and people's interaction with them through what P. Gupta (2019: 133–35) conceptualized as practices of 'renovation' based on her fieldwork in Beira.

In this book, I seek to understand how Mpatamatu's residents accommodated the ruinous structural changes in their living environment from the perspective of post-industrial, and more concretely post-paternalistic, ruination and renovation. How did processes of ruination unfold in Mpatamatu, and what were their local characteristics? These characteristics prompt my central question: What did people do about what they were left with? This question is related to two more issues that concern Mpatamatu as a material living environment: How was the abandoned corporate materiality brought back into unison with the changing social life of the township? And how was Mpatamatu repositioned in relation to the outside world?

I offer an analysis of how Mpatamatu's residents refigured the township's corporate remains and how the relationships between certain social groups changed in the face of the reappropriations of the former social welfare buildings. I retrace the material dimension of social relations in Mpatamatu's corporate past and relate it to the social realities that unfold the buildings' material present. In contrast to many other mining sites on Zambia's Copperbelt and elsewhere in southern Africa, in Mpatamatu practices of corporate paternalism were not succeeded by practices of corporate social responsibility (CSR).

The context of my central argument is the complete dissolution of a central corporate structure into individual private projects. The former social welfare buildings became sites of relocation, renovation, reintegration and reconnection. Contrary to the disappearance of corporate paternalism from the township, these sites were used to formulate a normativity that was reminiscent of a paternalist past in the face of a neoliberal present. Theoretically, I seek to contribute to the conceptualization of the interrelatedness between corporate paternalism, post-paternalist ruination and human agency in processes of renovation. I show how paternalist dependence was reinvented by the residents of Mpatamatu as a response to the absence of CSR practices by the local mining company. Ultimately, this ethnography pushes the conceptual boundaries of 'ruination' further and engages with the question of structural bias in the analysis of human action.

The concept of 'ruination' made it possible for me to capture the social experiences that were related to Mpatamatu's social welfare buildings, the township's material decay and its residents' loss of social status. The processual character of this concept was able to recognize the durability of the corporate-paternalist dimension in the living environment of Mpatamatu's residents. During my training as a historian of China, I was taught to be critical of dynastic watersheds and their supposed discontinuities.[1] 'Ruination' allowed me to follow up Macmillan's (2012: 548) question of 'what happens *after mining*' without detaching it from Mpatamatu's history as a corporate mine township. What people did about the

Figure 0.1. The signposts and metal arch welcoming the visitor to Luanshya. Photo by the author.

corporate remains they were left with had something to do with how they had lived under corporate paternalism. To me, the answers to my questions were to be found in the social dependencies that were inscribed in the material buildings when the township was first established; in the buildings' materiality, which remained a part of the residents' living environment after the copper sector was reprivatized; in the projects of renovation that took place in the township's former social welfare buildings; and in a neoliberal policy that had failed to integrate Mpatamatu into the CSR measures being implemented elsewhere in today's extractive industries (Rajak 2011: 8).

Entering Luanshya

Labelled a 'ghost town' after the privatization of Zambia Consolidated Copper Mines (ZCCM) in 1997 and the ensuing mass retrenchments in the early 2000s (Arndt 2010; Kaunda 1999), Luanshya in 2015/2016 did not present itself to me at all as an empty town. Interested in China–Africa relations, I first approached the mining town in Zambia's Copperbelt Province as a site of Chinese overseas investment.

In 2009, the Chinese state-owned company China Nonferrous Metal Mining (Group) Corporation (CNMC), listed under the State-owned Assets Supervision

and Administration Commission of the State Council of the People's Republic of China (SASAC),[2] took over the local copper mine in what was the latter's third change of ownership since the sector was reprivatized (Katasefa 2009; Shacinda 2009). CNMC Luanshya Copper Mines (CLM) was the state corporation's third major investment after the mine in Chambishi run by Non-Ferrous China-Africa (NFCA) and the Zambia–China Economic and Trade Cooperation Zone (ZCCZ), which included a newly constructed copper smelter (CNMC 2011).

CNMC's holding companies on the Copperbelt are part of a larger picture of Chinese investments in Zambia. Since the 2000s, a steady flow of Chinese individuals has arrived in the country (Guo Chatelard 2011; Postel 2017). As economic actors, these individuals have entered almost all sectors of the Zambian economy, from mining to logistics, construction, agriculture and tourism. A 2015 list compiled by China's Ministry of Commerce (MOFCOM) comprised more than five hundred Chinese companies in Zambia, while a list compiled by Zambia's National Council for Construction of the same year is dominated by Chinese companies in the infrastructure sector.[3] The presence of 'China in Zambia' has been a public and political issue since Michael Sata's anti-Chinese election campaign in 2006.[4]

When I entered Luanshya from the north through its iconic metal arch (see Figure 0.1), at first I could not find any CLM signs in the parade of billboards welcoming me to the town. On the contrary, I immediately became immersed in Luanshya's history as a place of industrial copper mining before and after Zambia's independence. On top of the metal arch rested the town's coat of arms. It showed a serpent in the claws of an eagle and two roan antelopes supporting a shield. All the animals wore an *ankh* necklace. Also depicted were two golden crowns on a blue background above red scales on a golden background, and a golden pick on a red background. Below it was written in Latin *aes erat in pretio*, 'copper was prized then'.[5]

In an instant, the history of Luanshya as a mining town built under British colonialism in Central Africa was unfolded in front of me (see Chapter 1). The city 'came into being to serve Roan Antelope [Copper Mining]' (Gann 1964: 211). It was no 'isolated colonial mining outpost' but part of 'a belt of towns with heavy industry' (Potts 2005: 584). The serpent alluded to the 'Luanshya snake story', a story about the high death toll due to tropical disease and Lamba opposition to the sinking of a mine during the early days of the town as a mining camp. There was the narrative of a roan antelope being shot to 'discover' the riches of the ground, represented by the Egyptian hieroglyph symbolizing copper. The antelope subsequently lent its name to the mine. The scales and pick stood for the twin character of Luanshya, consisting of the corporate-mining and government-municipal parts of the town (Smith 1985: 1490–92). Luanshya was born when 'copper was prized' in the late 1920s and, so it seemed, could only thrive in times of demand for the metal.

The *chitenge*, a fabric usually worn and used by women, waving beneath the coat of arms brought me back to Zambia's political present. It bore the colours of the ruling party, the Patriotic Front (PF), and also carried a portrait of the late president, Michael Sata (1937–2014). In 2015/2016, his successor Edgar Lungu was still reliant on Sata's agenda and reputation as a charismatic, sharp-tongued leader nicknamed 'King Cobra'. Luanshya's two constituencies were in the hands of PF candidates Steven Chungu and Chishimba Kambwili. The town's green decoration before the August 2016 elections made a claim to the PF's dominance. It turned out to be a tight race for the presidency between the incumbent, President Lungu, and his United Party for National Development (UPND) opponent Hakainde Hichilema (ECZ 2016). The election campaign had been overshadowed by violence and ever-changing political alliances (Branson 2016; Laterza and Mususa 2015).

Among the signboards, a guest house and a lodge welcomed the visitor to Luanshya. A distributor of second-hand Japanese spare parts and cars, omnipresent on Zambia's roads, also sought attention. South African banks were looking for potential customers. Metal Fabricators of Zambia (ZAMEFA), representing one of the few forward linkages extending from copper extraction into manufacturing, marked its plant's location in town.[6] The billboard of the Electoral Commission of Zambia and the uncountable election posters hiding the ruinous state of the former checkpoint shelters joined the *chitenge* above in pointing to the political significance of 2016 as an election year.

On the back of one of the shelters below the metal arch, amidst the election posters of the PF, UPND, Rainbow Party and independents, stood the letters 'CNMC LUANSHYA'. At last I had found a trace of the Chinese company's presence in Luanshya. It was common on the Copperbelt for mining companies to sponsor checkpoints and bus shelters. After CLM placed its underground operations into maintenance in September 2015 (Wangwe 2015), the company's reputation had been damaged. It was politics that increased its local presence, from PF's dominance in campaigning to Hichilema's appearance in the Luanshya court right after the elections.[7]

A metal structure commemorating Zambia's 42nd anniversary of independence in 2006, covered with the remains of a burnt banner celebrating its 50th anniversary in 2014, and a signboard to the city's outdated website pointed to the financial constraints of the Luanshya municipality. Changing mine operators meant unstable municipal revenues. A project sign of the Ministry of Local Government and Housing revealed that the town's water supply and sanitation remained a problem since their infrastructures had been passed on from the corporation to the municipal authorities, as was underlined by the defunct street lights.

The Rotary Club's signboard in turn was indicative of the fact that many previously corporate and government responsibilities had been handed over to private charity initiatives. Burnt grass on the roadside hinted at the heat of Zambia's dry season. Dust and garbage occasionally crossed the tarmac road, which had seen better days. A lorry driver was taking a break before moving on and joining the fleet on Zambia's roads that kept the country's economy alive.

Mpatamatu is situated far from the main arteries of the copper industry (see Map 0.2): off the national highway T3 that extends T2, connecting the capital Lusaka with major Copperbelt towns like Ndola, Kitwe and Chingola, off the main road running from T3 southwards through Luanshya towards Mpongwe and beyond the former mine township of Roan. Detached from the sometimes heated atmosphere of Luanshya on the outskirts of town lay 'the place where the boats got stuck' (see Figure 0.2; RMMTMB 1978).[8]

Mpatamatu was located in a three-fold periphery off the beaten track. The township marked Luanshya's final outpost on the edge of the Muliashi open pit mine. Beyond it was the Miombo forest, indigenous savannah woodlands. On a windy day at the end of the dry season, dust rose over the township as high as the spray of the Mosi-oa-Tunya in Livingstone during the rainy season. In contrast to the country's number one national monument and World Heritage Site, few people visited Mpatamatu. Whenever President Lungu visited, roads needed to be fixed, and ultimately he did not stay long.[9]

The more I learned about Mpatamatu and its residents, the more it emerged that this particular place was related to my own biography. It turned out that the Max Planck Institute for Social Anthropology that supported my research proj-

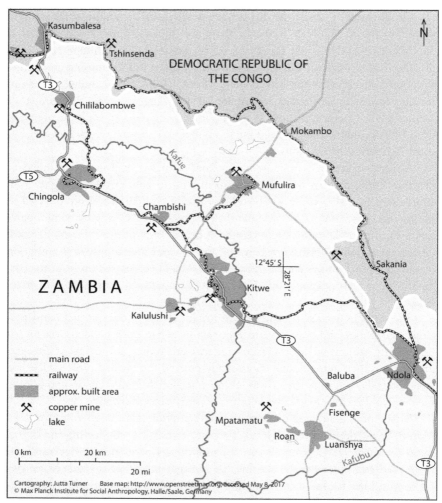

Map 0.2. Zambia's Copperbelt with its most important towns and mines on both sides of its border with the Democratic Republic of the Congo (DRC). Jutta Turner (Max Planck Institute for Social Anthropology, Halle/Saale).

ect on the Copperbelt was itself located fifty kilometres east of a former copper mining area, known as *Mansfelder Land* (Spilker 2010). I came to understand that the copper mining areas of the world formed what Anderson (2006: 33–36) called an 'imagined community'.[10] Mines actively related to each other, for example, by writing about other mines in their company magazines. To my great astonishment, a 1959 article in Roan Antelope Copper Mines' (RACM) company magazine *Horizon* on 'Copper and the Postage Stamp' included stamps from the German Democratic Republic (GDR) celebrating the 750th anniversary of *Mansfelder Kupfer*, copper from Mansfeld (Rhodian 1959: 16).

The Max Planck Institute was also fifteen kilometres north of the chemical plant formerly known as 'Buna' in Schkopau.[11] The plant had been founded by the Interessen-Gemeinschaft Farbenindustrie, a German chemical conglomerate known as IG Farben, in the second half of the 1930s. After the Second World War, Buna became the backbone of the GDR's plastics industry. The paternalistic care of this 'people's enterprise' – in German, *Volkseigener Betrieb* (VEB) – formed the basis for the lives of tens of thousands of workers. Among them was my maternal grandfather, who joined Buna as a chemist in 1959 and was allocated a house in the *Doktoren-*

Figure 0.2. Roan Mpatamatu Mine Township Management Board's coat of arms. ZCCM-IH Archives, Ndola.

siedlung, the 'doctors' quarters'. Irrespective of the GDR's ideological claims, Buna had taken over the spatial segregation of different parts of the labour force from its predecessor, a phenomenon common in Copperbelt mining towns.

A peculiarity of corporate paternalism in socialist countries like the GDR was one type of social welfare building: the *Kulturhaus* (Hain and Stroux 1996; Hartung 1997). These 'culture houses' offered a variety of cultural programmes to workers and their dependants. They reminded me of the community centres in Mpatamatu. Hence, like many of my research participants, my mother grew up in the shadow of a large corporate enterprise that set the boundaries for what was attainable and what was not, what was possible and what remained impossible (see Figure 0.3).

Reprivatization, corporate abandonment, ruination and renovation since 1995/1997 changed the living environments in Schkopau and Mpatamatu respectively.[12] In both places, corporate housing was sold to its existing tenants. In Schkopau this resulted in a renovation boom that relegated houses that had become grey from carbide sediments to the past. People in Mpatamatu started private businesses in the former mine houses. However, Buna's *Kulturhaus* deteriorated into a state of a ruin, having

Figure 0.3. The author's mother in an arts class at Buna's *Haus der Freundschaft*, 1968. Photo provided by the author's mother.

been closed by the authorities and fenced off. In contrast, there was not a single former social welfare building in Mpatamatu that remained unused in this township of twenty thousand people when I conducted fieldwork there in 2016.

Engaging Relations

When Burawoy revisited his fieldwork on African advancement in Zambia's copper industry, he came to realize that his methods violated the principles of what he termed 'positive science' (Burawoy 1998: 10). His reflections followed earlier interventions positioning ethnography against the hypothesis-testing sciences (Agar 1996: 113–31). On the Copperbelt, Burawoy disregarded 'reactivity' because he did nothing to avoid affecting his field site and based his fieldwork on social engagement instead. He also violated the principle of 'reliability' in the selection of his data. The practices of everyday life he wanted to observe kept on changing, making the 'replicability' of his data impossible, as his findings were mainly dependent on him being an engaged ethnographer. Finally, he was left with the question of whether his particular observations were in any sense 'representative' of the phenomenon under scrutiny, namely African industrial advancement, whether in his own case or beyond it (Burawoy 1998: 10–11).

Burawoy (1998: 14–16) concluded that he had been working under a different model of science, not 'positive' but 'reflexive', and therefore defined by different principles. Burawoy's engagement with a social phenomenon in a particular field site led to an 'intervention'. My interaction with the residents of Mpatamatu formed the basis for my understanding of the role the former social welfare buildings had played in people's lives and how the buildings were being used at the time of my fieldwork. Burawoy had followed his participants in space and time, aggregating social situations into a social 'process'. My investigation included observations of Mpatamatu's material and social present and a restructuring of the township's past. I participated in and witnessed different situations in and around the former social welfare buildings. This enabled me to identify different aspects of a process of social change in Mpatamatu. The process included the recent reappropriation of the buildings after Mpatamatu had been abandoned by the mine.

Burawoy realized that the local was shaped by forces external to his field site and vice versa, that is, that there was a reciprocal constitutive relationship between the 'local' and the 'global' (Massey 2012: 101). He needed to look at the everyday world from the perspective of its 'structuration'. The access difficulties I encountered in the first half of my fieldwork had already revealed the complexity of my field site's structuration as a site of copper extraction (Straube 2020), a town still reliant on its mine, a part of the country's most important industrial hub, the home of numerous urban voters, and a site of Chinese state-corporate overseas investment in Africa.

Finally, Burawoy saw the contribution of a particular case not in its representativeness, but in how far it contributed to the 'reconstruction' of theory. Processes of material and social ruination may look different in other former mine townships on the Copperbelt or other post-industrial places around the world. However, my data from Mpatamatu entered a dialogue with existing theorizations of corrosive processes of ruination and of the translations of corporate paternalist practices into CSR measures. Specifically, the case of Mpatamatu allowed me to conceptually unpack the penetration of ruination with projects of creative renovation and the relationship between corporate paternalism and private reappropriation from the perspective of human agency.

Burawoy (1998: 16–22) closed his treatise on reflexive science with a return to a method previously developed in the discipline of social anthropology by the scholars of the Rhodes-Livingstone Institute (RLI) and the Manchester School, 'the extended case method'.[13] This method extended social situations into social processes, and located them in power relations through the latter's operation in the former two. Consequently, social processes allowed the researcher to extend out to the forces that originated outside the field site where the social situations had been observed. However, fieldwork in general and the method in particular included a practical intrusion: an engaged ethnographer was an object in the local operation of power relations, too. This fact constituted a constraint in fieldwork. 'Power effects', that is, domination, silencing, objectification and normalization, required awareness and reflection (Burawoy 1998: 22–25).

Extending out, in my understanding, resulted in an explanatory proposal in order to comprehend social phenomena and the forces that gave rise to them. It denominated a process of interpretation which Reed (2011: 7–10, 89–121), based on Geertz (2006: 412–54), suggested was a separate 'epistemic mode' of theory-making in the human sciences.[14] My investigation of material and social ruination and renovation in Mpatamatu examined 'arrangements of signification and representation, the layers of social meaning, the shape of human experience' (Reed 2011: 10). These arrangements had to be observed in concrete social situations. Among the questions that guided me through interviews were: What did the collapse of corporate paternalism mean to mineworker families? What did the social welfare buildings represent for government, company and residents? How did residents experience corporate paternalism and abandonment? What motivated them in their renovative practices?

Burawoy's and Reed's thoughts on epistemology offered an entry point to how I reflected upon my positionality in the field. I pursued a variety of methods around a core of ethnographic fieldwork. This included participant observation in the former social welfare buildings, sometimes crystallizing in moments of what Rosaldo termed 'deep hanging out' (Clifford 1997: 188, endnote 2, 219). I engaged in conversations and conducted interviews, open, biographical and semi-structured, with the sitting tenants of former social welfare buildings and

Mpatamatu's residents. Both conversations and interviews always remained 'informal' in Agar's (1996: 140) sense, leaving situations negotiable on my research participants' terms. Usually, informal encounters were scheduled in instances of 'ethnography by appointment' (Desjarlais 2003: 18). These instances and my presence during a day's fieldwork always resulted in continuous follow-up situations of ethnographic enquiry. My main field site was the township of Mpatamatu in the city of Luanshya, which I explored on foot. I also conducted complementary interviews in the neighbouring Roan township, downtown Luanshya, Baluba, Kitwe, the provincial capital Ndola and the national capital Lusaka.

I divided my research participants into four 'experience cohorts'.[15] In following P. Gupta (2019: 130), I realized that the residents of Mpatamatu lived in a material environment and experienced social time as linked to different periods of the mine's history: colonial (1900–1964), corporate-paternalist (1927–1997), state-socialist (1970–1991) and neoliberal (since 1997). I came to understand Mpatamatu in the context of its inhabitants' experiences through de Certeau's (1988: 201) concept of a 'stratified place' that represented a 'whole made up of pieces that are not contemporary and still linked to totalities that have fallen to ruins'.

My first cohort of research participants comprised men who had been former mineworkers in Luanshya as early as the late 1960s. Some of them dropped out of ZCCM before 1997, and many were retrenched after Roan Antelope Mining Corporation of Zambia (RAMCOZ) became bankrupt in 2000. A minority managed to remain in the service of the successive mine operators up to CLM or one of its subcontractors such as China 15th Metallurgical Construction Group Corporation (15MCC). This cohort provided the most intricate knowledge of mine township life under corporate paternalism, needless to say from a male insider's perspective, and against the backdrop of corporate abandonment and, quite often, personal social ruination after the mine's reprivatization.

The second cohort was made up of women who came to Luanshya to accompany their husbands in the first cohort or to find work themselves. These women arrived as early as the 1970s and provided the gender counterpart to the first cohort's body of knowledge. They recalled the kinds of positions the mining company envisaged for women under corporate paternalism and explained to me what positions they actually occupied at the time of my fieldwork in contrast to that era.

The third cohort consisted of men who grew up as sons or dependants in mineworker families headed by the first and second cohort in Mpatamatu in the late 1980s and early 1990s. They experienced corporate paternalism in the form of after-school leisure facilities, but most prominently the absence of these facilities after ZCCM's privatization.

Finally, the fourth cohort comprised men who worked in Mpatamatu before and after ZCCM's privatization, however not as mineworkers, but as teachers. These men provided an occupational counterpart to the men of the first cohort.

They had been marked by their subaltern status as government employees in a mine township built for mineworkers under corporate paternalism. At the time of my fieldwork, this cohort was characterized by social promotion and increased economic action within the residential community of Mpatamatu.

I extended my biographical approach towards my research participants to the social welfare buildings. I tried to identify traces of different periods of social experience inscribed in them. This biographical interrogation of the buildings was based on an approach proposed by Kopytoff (2011: 64) in Appadurai's seminal volume *The Social Life of Things*. In following Dawdy (2010: 768–69), I recognized that '[ruins] and dilapidated, adaptively reused buildings [were] architectural equivalents of Benjamin's outmoded commodities', merchandise he had come to see as 'semiotic vessels' during his famous observations at the arcades (Benjamin 2002: 466). The social welfare buildings were such vessels with regard to the mining company's presence in Mpatamatu, the relationship of particular social groups, and the role the buildings played in residents' lives.

The people of Mpatamatu and the social welfare buildings formed a community that I was only to understand through their 'inter-relationality', the changing linkages producing the community that both comprised material and social relations of meaning (Studdert and Walkerdine 2016: 19, 28, footnote 1). Following Myhre's revisit of 'Strathern's idea . . . that the relation simultaneously connects and divides', the social welfare buildings constitute the 'things where connections are severed and networks cut' (Myhre 2016: 2). The changing relations between Mpatamatu's residents and the buildings as well as their meaning for the relations between the experience cohorts introduced above reset the entire community. Social change interacted directly with material change.

I supplemented my fieldwork with tours to Mpatamatu's former social welfare buildings guided by my interlocutors. These visits centred on the buildings themselves. They often triggered social knowledge through the fact of my own presence at the building with my research participants: looking at a building, its construction materials and surrounding environment from the outside, and getting an impression of the rooms and spatial dimensions from the inside. I documented these tours with drawings and photography.

Over time, I grasped the township in its spatial extensiveness and infrastructural condition. I systematically collected geographical data on the location of the former social welfare buildings and the spatial arrangements of the township's sections using a global positioning system (GPS) device. This included data on the course of streets and footpaths, surface materials, streams and buildings. I compared this information with historical maps I found in the archives. The product of this mapping process is openly accessible online. Map 0.1 is a graphically enhanced township map based on OpenStreetMap (2016).

My investigation into the history of Mpatamatu and its former social welfare buildings included research in several archives. I started this process by looking at the records stored at the RAMCOZ Receiver's Office in Luanshya. The main part of my archival work took place in the ZCCM-IH Archives in Ndola. Eventually, the corporate history of the Roan Selection Trust (RST) led me to the London School of Economics and Political Science (LSE) Library Archives. I supplemented my work in the archives with online research, for example to track down the development agreements sealing ZCCM's privatization, the careers of Collings and Schaerer as town planners and the history of the contractors who built Mpatamatu.

Researching Luanshya

Conducting fieldwork on foot enabled me to move around Mpatamatu in the way its residents did. Most of them had no car, and few possessed a bicycle. Some time into my fieldwork I heard *muzungu bele*, literally 'not a real White person',[16] being shouted at me in Mpatamatu. My research participants disagreed on how to interpret this characterization. Some suggested that it had to do with my dark hair, while others pointed to the fact that I walked on foot in the township, something a 'real' *muzungu*, a cross-Bantu term for White persons, never did.

The ethnographic practice of walking around the township on foot helped me to cut across ensuing power hierarchies. It created moments of encounter that led to so many conversations and insights. However, it did not change the fact that I was in a 'dominating' position (Burawoy 1998: 22–23), a position I was not used to and was anxious about. I was living at a higher socio-economic level than most of the people around me. I came from and would return to a country that was considered wealthy, a country that was at the centre of international attention in the wake of the 2015/2016 refugee migration crisis from Syria to Europe. Consequently, I was regarded as being fortunate or, as one of the workers on the farm where I lived with my family put it, '*Mwakulaenda na malāki!*': 'wherever you go, you will find luck'.

My experience confirmed Schumaker's conclusion that fieldwork itself was 'politicized' and that the field was 'a constructed and negotiated space for the production of knowledge' (Schumaker 2001: 187, 227). My original research proposal had been an enquiry into Chinese–Zambian social encounters in the context of copper mining. After six months networking with CLM's management through Zambian ministries, their departments and two embassies without success, I realigned my research topic. Fieldwork access and its denial were a recurring topic in Copperbelt research (Straube 2020).

I arrived in Zambia thirty years after Ferguson (1999: xv) had conducted his fieldwork in 1985/1986. Research in and on the city of Luanshya had been conducted before and since, covering a range of classic anthropological issues, from social change to labour and women. Table 0.1 provides an overview of anthropologists who chose Luanshya as a field site.[17] Their contributions raised

Table 0.1. Luanshya as an ethnographic field site.

Years	Researcher	Main research focus
1953–1954	Epstein	Social change and the political representation of labour migrants
	Powdermaker	Social change and mass media
1963–1965	Harries-Jones	Social change and marital disputes, UNIP's rise in corporate mine townships
1978	Chauncey	Social change and women's labour
1982–1983	Mijere	Unionism and nationalism on the Copperbelt
1991–1992	Schumaker	RLI research and fieldwork
2001–2002		Corporate town planning and medical history
2007–2010	Mususa	Social change on the post-reprivatization Copperbelt

my interest and were instrumental in my own understanding of the place and of social life in Mpatamatu.

Next to these anthropological studies, all based on long-term ethnographic fieldwork in Luanshya, other research projects included field visits to the town and interviews with its residents. They helped me reconstruct the history of Luanshya and identify the structural changes in people's lives before and after the copper industry's reprivatization in 1997. Among these are Mitchell (1954) on urbanization in 1951, Perrings (1979) on Zambian labour history in 1975, Parpart (1983, 1986a, 1986b) on women in 1976, Larmer (2004) on mineworker unionism and historical research in 2002/2003, Kazimbaya-Senkwe, Mwila and Guy (2007) on water domestication in 2005, Tembo (2009) on health care and Smart (2014) on urban agriculture in 2011.

My interest in the history of Luanshya led me to realize that written accounts of the former mining town were still in the hands of the industry, namely the receivership of the first post-reprivatization mine operator RAMCOZ in Luanshya and ZCCM-IH's Archives in Ndola. Employees at the receiver's office helped me to understand the process of separating mining-related assets from so-called 'non-core social assets'. It was here that I obtained a list of the Luanshya Municipal Council (LMC), which directed my attention to the former social welfare buildings of Mpatamatu (LMC 1991). At a time when I was forced to accept CLM's denial of research permission, I got to know a resident of Mpatamatu by the name of Felix Chanda. He had grown up in the township and introduced me to its inhabitants.

From April to October 2016, I carried out fieldwork in Mpatamatu. In retrospect, with the confident feeling of having a story to tell about the township, its former social welfare buildings and its residents, I often asked myself why I did not abandon my initial project earlier and why I was so persistent in trying to gain fieldwork access to one of CNMC's mines. I came to realize that my work in Mpatamatu was only possible because of this initial idea. The path dependency of my research project became even clearer when I looked at the time I was acquainted with the person who introduced me to Mpatamatu. In short, my research chronology substantiated the 'item of folklore' that Agar (1986: 15) pointed to when reflecting on ethnography: 'anthropologists are (in)famous at granting agencies for proposing one study and returning with another'.

Structuring a Book

In this book, I seek to answer the question of what people in Mpatamatu did with the corporate remains that were left by the mine when ZCCM was broken up in 1997. This question touches upon the material environment of the township, the changing social relations inhabiting it, and the relationship between the material and the social. In this sense, I consider the former social welfare buildings to be material aspects of social life in Mpatamatu. The following chapters focus on particular social relations of agonism that serve as entry points to my study of how the former social welfare buildings were reappropriated. They make visible which particular connections between the social and the material were cut and reset. I retrace how these relations of agonism changed over time and how this transition interacted with the buildings. From being integral parts of corporate paternalism, the social welfare buildings became sites of independent social projects restructuring social life in Mpatamatu.

In Chapter 1, 'Of Company and Government', I retrace the history of Luanshya as a mining town and Mpatamatu as a mine township. The chapter follows the practices performed by corporate capital and colonial government in seeking to create a 'stable' industrial setting. This was an environment in which the company could exploit the territory's natural and human resources. The government supplied the legal framework and otherwise absorbed some of the mining companies' revenues. I attempt to establish how the social welfare buildings first came into existence and how they were used by the township residents under corporate paternalism. The chapter ends by describing the disintegration of this paternalistic setting in a process of corporate abandonment. Mpatamatu's former social welfare buildings were left to fall into ruin.

Chapter 2, 'Of Men and Women', follows the establishment of the mine township as a miners' place ruled by domestic patriarchy and corporate paternalism. I look at how a specific class of social welfare building, the community centres, were intended to shape the relationship between mining men and dependent women. I investigate how women both complied with and challenged this socio-economic hierarchy and material environment. I show how the mass retrenchments of the early 2000s affected mineworkers' lives and how women replaced men as the main economic contributors to the family household.

In the third chapter, 'Of Miners and Teachers', I address the exclusiveness of Mpatamatu as a corporate mine township in relation to teachers working at the township's government schools. Starting with the case of Mpatamatu's first clinic for government workers, I show how the township started to dissolve as an exclusive company town. I revisit the community centres where teachers had become the main sitting tenants after ZCCM's privatization. I retrace how teachers replaced mineworkers in the social welfare buildings, protected these buildings in the face of economic decline, and reintegrated them into the community of Mpatamatu.

In Chapter 4, 'Of Miners and Preachers', I examine the history of leisure in Mpatamatu. I look at beer halls, clubs and the township's sports facilities as corporate provisions for mineworkers. I introduce churches as opposing locations where residents went after work. I follow Pentecostal congregations in their conversion of former leisure facilities into houses of prayer. Moreover, I tell the story of how some mineworkers themselves became preachers. The chapter completes my investigation of how Mpatamatu's social welfare buildings turned from a centrally controlled part of corporate infrastructure into independent private social projects.

In the concluding chapter, 'Things Reassembled', I revisit the findings of each chapter and relate them to my central question of how ruination and renovation in Mpatamatu unfolded. By identifying four socio-material processes in Mpatamatu, namely relocation, renovation, reintegration and reconnection, I propose an answer to what people did about what they were left with and how material reappropriation and social change were related to each other in the absence of CSR practices and government support. I show how processes of ruination converge with processes of renovation in the interaction between materiality and human agency.

Notes

1. For the classic study of China's 'watershed' year of 1949, see Cohen (2003).
2. CNMC's name in Chinese is *Zhongguo youse kuangye jituan youxian gongsi* 中国有色矿业集团有限公司. See SASAC (2020).
3. See MOFCOM (2015) and National Council for Construction (2015). The MOFCOM list is no longer online. I suspect, in fact, that it was an internal list that was put online by mistake. It included manager names and phone numbers.
4. See Sautman (2013), Larmer and Fraser (2007) and Schatz (2006).
5. The full verse from Ovid's *Fasti* reads *aes erat in pretio, chalybeia massa latebat*, 'copper was prized then, iron was still hidden'. See Kline (2004).
6. ZAMEFA was owned by the US company General Cable at the time of my fieldwork. In late 2016 it was taken over by Circuit Breaker Industries Electric, owned by Reunert Limited from South Africa.
7. Hichilema and his deputy were charged with 'seditious practices and unlawful assembly'. See *Lusaka Times* (2016).

8. The name 'Mpatamatu' is from Lamba, one of the many Bantu languages spoken in Zambia: *m-* signifies a location, *-pata* means 'to stick' and *amato* is the plural form of *ubwato*, 'ship'. The name points to the Mpata Hills west of the township with its many little seasonal streams, tributaries of the Kafue river on which people travelled by boat in the past.

9. During a 2017 visit, Lungu allotted twenty-five minutes for the entire city of Luanshya. He only drove through the townships of Roan and Mpatamatu. See Chileshe (2017).

10. Anderson (2006: 33–36) considered the 'mass ceremony' of reading newspapers to be the crux of the link between one's own everyday practices and a wider 'imagined community'. Corporate magazines fulfilled this task for mining companies and their labour force. See also Rajak (2011: 47).

11. 'Buna' is composed of *bu*tadiene and sodium, lat. *na*trium, and is a synonym for synthetic rubber, the plant's main product.

12. Buna was sold to the US company Dow Chemicals in 1998; see Dow (2018).

13. See Handelman (2006), with reference to Gluckman's (1940) paradigmatic article based on an extended case study.

14. Reed (2011) calls the other two of the total three epistemic modes 'realist' (Chapter 2: Reality) and 'normative' (Chapter 3: Utopia).

15. On 'experience cohorts' in the context of mining in southern Africa, see Jønsson and Bryceson (2014: 33).

16. I follow Arndt and Hornscheidt (2009: 13–14) by capitalizing both 'Black' and 'White' in order to identify them as political concepts. They refer primarily not to skin colour but to positions within uneven relations of power that need to be both reflected on and changed.

17. See Epstein (1958), Powdermaker (1962), Harries-Jones (1964, 1975), Chauncey (1981), Mijere (1985), Schumaker (2001, 2008) and Mususa (2014).

Chapter 1

Of Company and Government

On 18 April 1890, Joseph Thomson (1858–1895) set out from England to travel to the Cape. After receiving final instructions from Cecil Rhodes (1853–1902) in person, he sailed on as a British South Africa Company (BSAC) agent to Quelimane on the Mozambique Channel. On 26 June, his party continued by boat inland up the Zambezi River. He passed Blantyre in July and moved up the Shire to Lake Nyasa, reaching the Luangwa Valley at the beginning of September. Initially, he was sent to Lake Bangweulu. However, his caravan, plagued by sickness, stopped short at the southern tip of the Bangweulu wetlands at around latitude 12° south. Travelling on the Luapula River, he reoriented the enterprise to advance on the Kafue valley. The river's upper course runs through the area that is today known as Zambia's Copperbelt. Thomson failed to reach the Kafue. On 4 November 1890, his party arrived at Lamba Chief Mshiri's village, after becoming stranded on the Lunsemfwa River at longitude 29° east. His porters objected to moving further west, and Thomson fell sick. The smallpox, most probably brought in by his party, killed Chief Mshiri's son. Thomson was forced to abandon his mission and returned to Lake Nyasa only two weeks later (Thomson 1893: 97–113). However, those two weeks were not without consequence for the place that came to be known by the name of Luanshya.

Thomson returned from his expedition with fourteen treaties signed by local chiefs between September and November 1890 (Faber 1971a: 138–39; Krishnamurthy 1969: 590). The treaty concluded with Chief Mshiri complemented the Lochner Concession, signed by King Lewanika of Barotseland (Letcher 1932: 60; Siegel 1989: 2), in establishing the 'legal' basis for the BSAC's colonizing authority over mineral rights in an area that was to become the British protectorate of Northern Rhodesia in 1924 and Zambia in 1964. The concessions granted to mining companies by the BSAC had their roots in the extraction of 'exclusive private property rights (exclusive, that is, to the colonizers)' from local authorities (Home 2015: 56). Among the four treaties Thomson signed with Lamba chiefs, it is particularly that concluded with Chief Mshiri that made claims to these 'exclusive' rights and unfolded legal potential with regard to Luanshya and the copper ore in its soil (Krishnamurthy 1969: 594). The treaty read:

> Treaty between MSHIRI Chief of Southern Iramba [Lamba] occupying the Upper Lusefwa [Lunsemfwa] River basin and Joseph Thomson in his capacity as representative of the British South Africa Company hereinafter called the Company.
>
> On the 6th November 1890 in the presence of the headmen and people of Southern Iramba Mshiri the Chief hereby agrees for himself his heirs and successors and on behalf of his people:
>
> (1) To accept the British Flag and to place himself irrevocably under the Protectorate of Great Britain.
>
> (2) To grant to the Company the sole right to search, prospect, exploit, dig for and keep all minerals and metals.
>
> (3) To grant the sole right to construct, improve, equip, work, manage and control all kinds of public works and conveniences of general and public utility and to give to the Company absolutely and exclusively all commercial privileges of whatsoever kind.
>
> (4) Mshiri further concedes to the Company the right to do all such things as are incidental or conducive to the exercise, attainment or protection of all or any of the rights, powers and concessions hereby granted.
>
> (5) Mshiri further agrees not to enter into any treaty or alliance with any other person, Company or state or to grant any concession of land without the consent of the Company in writing, it being understood that this covenant shall be considered in the light of a treaty between the said Chief and people and the Government of Her Britannic Majesty Queen Victoria.
>
> (6) These grants and concessions are to apply to the whole of Southern Iramba lying in the Upper Basin of the River Lusifwa one of the western tributaries of the Loangwa [Luangwa].
>
> In consideration of these grants and concessions the Company agrees to pay Mshiri on the signing of this treaty goods to the amount of £10 (ten pounds) and the annual sum of £20 (twenty pounds) to commence on practical advantage being taken of the commercial or mining clauses of this treaty.

JOSEPH THOMSON.
for the
BRITISH SOUTH AFRICA COMPANY.

Mshiri's mark
(Northern Rhodesia 1964: 12, cited in Faber 1971a: 135–36)

Many Copperbelt scholars have referred to the 'dubious' nature of Thomson's fourteen treaties.[1] Based on Faber's (1971a: 131, 134, 140–41) seminal article, I shall highlight four issues concerning this charge of dubiousness in the case of the treaty with Chief Mshiri quoted above.

First, despite carrying a geographical mark, the treaty's place of signature lay approximately two hundred kilometres east of the area that was to become 'the Copperbelt'. Second, while Mshiri was a Lamba chief, he had no jurisdiction over the area that would later be separated into claims and handed out as mining concessions. Third, the treaty was concluded only two days after Thomson's arrival in Chief Mshiri's village. This fact made 'the presence of the headmen and people', as noted in the preamble of the treaty, unlikely in light of contemporary modes of transportation. Finally, according to a relative of Chief Mshiri present during the meeting and quoted by Faber, the contract's actual implications were not discussed between the parties.

The dubious nature of Thomson's treaties did not just occur to scholars in retrospect: the BSAC's own employees testified that 'there is a lot of humbug about the original agreements' (Northern Rhodesia 1964: 13), and they questioned the treaties' legal authority. However, Rhodes and the BSAC succeeded in getting the treaties sanctioned by the British Foreign Office in 1894 (Krishnamurthy 1969: 599) and in converting, as Faber (1971a: 131) noted, 'these scraps of paper into the basis of a commercial success'.

Concluding treaties like the one above with local authorities, comprising such detailed claims to the land as set out in clause (2), illustrated what Home (2015: 56) called the BSAC's 'land grabbing exercise'. This 'exercise' was, in fact, a colonial practice, one that fell within 'a broader set of practices structured in dominance' that Stoler and McGranahan (2007: 8) saw at the core of what they termed 'imperial formations'. The concept fused the structural and practical aspects of power, which Victoria (2016: 249) has elaborated on in his distinction between 'power', that is, the power relations that capacitate an actor to produce society, and 'politics', that is, the actual practice of those relations of power. Stoler and McGranahan (2007: 8) humanize this practice of power by looking at 'imperial formations' as 'polities of dislocation, processes of dispersion, appropriation, and displacement'.

In this chapter, I unpack the 'imperial formation' that produced the treaty with Chief Mshiri and that built the foundations for the industrial mining of copper in places like Luanshya. The BSAC provided the basis for mining companies like Roan Antelope Copper Mines (RACM) to establish a capitalist extractive order. This order was rooted in practices of dislocating the landscape, dispersing autochthonous cosmologies, appropriating its workers' lives and displacing the Lamba people. As the chapter title suggests, I follow earlier works in their reconstruction of Copperbelt history as an interaction between capital in the form of the mining companies and the government (Butler 2007; Sklar 1975). However, I shall also address Lamba responses to the emerging industrial complex. I move on to investigate the town-planning models that shaped Luanshya's mine townships such as Mpatamatu. Finally, I draw attention to the corporate provisions of the mine in the form of social welfare buildings and show how they were abandoned after the reprivatization of Zambia's copper sector in 1997.

Corporate Colonialism

Under the BSAC, corporate colonialism culminated in the company's monopoly over mineral rights. When Northern Rhodesia became a British protectorate in 1924, the BSAC retained this monopoly, which was reconfirmed in 1950 (Sklar 1975: 11, 35–36). At independence in 1964, the Zambian state acquired the BSAC's mineral rights and replaced the company as the provider of mining grants and collector of royalties (Roberts 1976: 221–22). However, concessions that had previously been granted to mining companies by the BSAC could not be altered. The overall legal composition of Zambia's copper sector only changed with the nationalization of the mines in 1969/1970 (Sklar 1975: 29–34; Ushewokunze 1974: 79).

Before an industry could develop 'minerals and metals' in accordance with clause (2) of the treaty with Chief Mshiri, they needed to be located. Several versions of how the copper deposits in Luanshya were 'discovered' exist. Needless to say, the Lamba who lived in the area at the time knew about the ore underground, its artisanal extraction and processing.[2] In fact, prospectors like William Collier (1870–1943) relied on local knowledge to find bodies of ore. The most dominant narrative of the Roan claim's 'discovery' in what was to become the mine and town of Luanshya was based on an expedition Collier undertook in 1902.[3] In 1931, RACM's US-American financier Alfred Chester Beatty (1875–1968) retold the story at the American Institute of Mining, Metallurgy, and Petroleum Engineers as follows:

> Late in 1902, an English prospector named Collier, travelling in the N'Dola district, came upon some natives using a green powder for medicinal purposes. Closer examination of the powder revealed that it was ground-up malachite [a copper carbonate]. . . . Collier endeavoured to persuade the natives to tell him, where they obtained this medicine, but for long time without success, because of the general feeling among the

natives that they did not wish to reveal resources of their lands to the white man. Finally, however, he persuaded one of the elders to at least take him part way toward the place where the malachite was supposed to occur. . . . The next morning Collier proceeded up the Luanshya and was about to make camp late that afternoon when he saw a roan antelope buck standing in the grass a little farther up the river. Collier stalked the buck and knocked him out with his first shot. When he came to the place where the dead buck lay he noticed a small outcrop with malachite stain. (Beatty 1931a: 1; 1931b: 518)

What struck me during fieldwork in Luanshya was the tenaciousness with which this account survived. When I first entered the town, I looked for someone at the Civic Centre, Luanshya's town hall, who was familiar with the history of the town. I was directed to the District Education Standards Officer of the Ministry of Education. In our first conversation, he reproduced Collier's story above.[4] Later, I found out that this narrative had been cast into copper in the form of the 'Collier Monument', a national heritage site in Luanshya (Zambia National Heritage Conservation Commission 1989). Collier's 'discovery', an imperial practice of appropriation, had been materialized and monumentalized in a concrete structure (Milner-Thornton 2012: 18). Its 'specialized lexicons' still '[clung] to people, places, and things' (Stoler 2016: 20). The story of a White man 'discovering' the ore in an act of adventurism had been challenged and publicly called into question (Mukuwa 1981). However, the 'epistemological claim' (Stoler and McGranahan 2007: 11) of the colonial enterprise and the mining industry persisted.

The significance of Collier's expedition does not lie in the fact that he 'discovered' copper, but rather that he helped translate the ore's presence into something meaningful for extractive capitalism: marked claims, geological properties and information on ore concentrations, all of which were essential for industrial mining.[5] Apart from measuring the landscape, there was something else that brought about the development of the Copperbelt as an industrial hub: an infrastructure of transportation. In order to get the copper to market, a railway line was necessary. In this sense, 'infrastructure' as a 'technical system' (Larkin 2008: 5), located below (Latin *infra*) the industry's production facilities, was established. Its construction represented a huge challenge.

The landlocked Copperbelt was at least 1,400 kilometres from any coast. The region had to be connected to Cape Town, the transportation hub 3,000 kilometres south of the Copperbelt. By the time Collier made his 'discovery' in 1902, the Cape railway had reached Salisbury (now Harare in Zimbabwe). Gradually, it was extended northwards, reaching the Mosi-oa-Tunya and Kalomo in 1904, Broken Hill (now Kabwe) in 1906 and the Congolese border on the Copperbelt in 1909. Eventually, a branch line to Luanshya put the mining town on the network in 1929.[6] The Cape railway's connection to the capitalist and colonial enterprise revealed this particular infrastructure's 'fundamentally relational' character as it became 'infrastructure in relation to organized practices', as well as its 'embeddedness', which Star and Ruhleder (1996: 113) identified as one dimension of infrastructure.

Two more challenges arose, apart from connecting the Copperbelt to the global market: finding workable methods to extract low-grade ore below the water table, and decreasing the incidence of tropical diseases. The first challenge was met by Beatty, who had founded the Selection Trust in 1914. He had gained experience in the exploitation of low-grade copper deposits in Utah, United States, and became acquainted with Central Africa during his negotiations with King Leopold II of Belgium on behalf of the Guggenheims. Beatty's knowledge of how to extract low-grade copper deposits gave him an advantage over his competitors in southern Africa.[7] In 1927 he founded the mining company that was to exploit the deposits 'discovered' by Collier in Luanshya:

> From 1927 London metal prices took an upward turn giving added cause for confidence in the future of the industry, and in that year Chester Beatty's Selection Trust launched Roan Antelope Mining Copper Mines (RACM), the second of the major mining companies [next to Anglo American], to develop a deposit located on the Luanshya river. (Perrings 1979: 75)

The shores of the Luanshya River were not uninhabited. Beatty's economic venture was challenged by the local Lamba people. Moreover, claims to the land by the Lamba were themselves challenged by other local authorities (Schumaker 2008: 829–30). Evidently, the concession that was granted to RACM was not an unpopulated *terra nullius*, nor did the copper ore have to be 'discovered' because of a lucky shot from a European prospector's rifle. Some Lamba people resisted forced migration through the Watch Tower Movement, a religious movement rooted in the doctrine of Jehovah's Witnesses, albeit developing independently from them in Central Africa (Cross 1973: 275–79; Siegel 1988: 76–77).

Most prominently, the Lamba put forward their claim to the land by relating the high death toll at the mine caused by malaria in the late 1920s to the presence of a snake spirit in the Luanshya River that needed to be placated. This second challenge was met by Arthur Storke (1894–1949), Beatty's managing director on the Copperbelt, who sought professional advice in 1929 (Schumaker 2011: 406). However, irrespective of the ensuing anti-malarial campaign carried out by the Ross Institute for Tropical Diseases in London, 'a dramatic cleansing ceremony' took place in 1930, reported in RACM's company magazine *Horizon*:

> At the Roan Antelope mine, considerable difficulty was being experienced in recruiting and keeping workers because of a persistent rumour

of a monstrous snake in the Luanshya River. The place was held accursed by local Africans . . . . [J.E. 'Chirupula'] Stephenson [(1876–1957), a former BSAC administrator] was able to gather the local 'priests' and to supervise a dramatic cleansing ceremony which earned him gratitude of the mining company, plus the offer of a reward, which was declined. (Hobson 1961: 23)

According to the Lamba, the snake spirit was responsible for all the deaths, as it had 'wriggled through the shafts, spewing water and poisonous gas and causing cave-ins' (Siegel 2008: 8). As noted earlier, ore had to be mined from below the water table. Water presented a constant threat to mineworkers labouring underground. In comparison with Collier's 'discovery', Schumaker (2008: 829) concluded, 'prospectors' hunting stories [were] as supernatural as African stories of snake spirits . . .'. Each narrative had the purpose of substantiating claims to the land backed by a supernatural force.

The dissemination of Collier's story represented an imperial practice.[8] It was aimed at establishing what Stoler (2008a: 350) termed 'colonial (un)truths', namely that it was an act of nature that revealed the soil's riches for industrial extraction. Correspondingly, the narrative of the snake spirit operated as 'a ritual apparatus used by the Lamba "owners of the land" to retain power in the face of colonialism' (Schumaker 2008: 838). The 'dramatic cleansing ritual' had been staged by RACM to appease the Lamba and improve the mine's reputation because of its need for labour. The 'priests' who were to dispel the spirit from the Luanshya River had been paid (Schumaker 2008: 830). In fact, the ritual was a symbolic gesture based on the misconceived belief of C.F. Spearpoint, RACM's African personnel manager, and Malcolm Watson, the Ross Institute's malaria expert, that 'the snake was an African metaphor for malaria' (Schumaker 2011: 405).[9]

Above all, RACM did not seek ritual but technical solutions to eradicate malaria, and with it, the stories about snake spirits and their underlying claims to the land. Based on her seminal research on the Ross Institute's anti-malarial programme in Luanshya from 1929 to 1931, Schumaker (2008: 840) identified processes of 'medicalisation and industrialisation' in concrete technical practices. *Dambos*, 'low, treeless, marshy areas, with shallow pools and light shade provided by reeds and grass' (Schumaker 2011: 409), were drained. Bodies of standing water were oiled and wetlands filled with tailings (Dalzell 1953b). The landscape was dramatically reassessed through colonial epistemological claims in the interests of capital.[10]

The Copperbelt was defined as an 'extractive space' (Frederiksen 2010: 237). *Dambos*, which for the Lamba had represented gardens for agricultural use, became the 'key to the control of malaria' (Schumaker 2008: 832). Schumaker (2008: 834) found that the Ross Institute's scientists spoke about the landscape as having been 'cured'.[11] The subsequent drop in the incidence of malaria, from a peak of ninety-four malaria cases per thousand inhabitants per month during the rainy season of 1929/1930 to fifty during the following rainy season and twenty-seven the rainy season after that (Dalzell 1953a: 52), backed RACM's corporate health campaign (see also Utzinger et al. 2002). Despite everything, however, stories about a snake in the rivers around Luanshya survived. Both Schumaker's research participants in the early 2000s and the residents of Mpatamatu I met during fieldwork in 2016 made it clear that a spirit was still present in Luanshya's rivers.

The Lamba opposed RACM's operations with a counter-claim to the land and refused to work underground (Siegel 1989: 4). At the same time, they interacted economically with the mining sector by offering native beer, agricultural produce and domestic services to the mine's African workforce.[12] In Luanshya too, 'mining activities tend[ed] to integrate surrounding regions into a single economic sphere' (Godoy 1985: 207). This integration was hierarchical, and the Lamba were relegated to a subaltern position outside the mine townships. The 'medical vision' behind the anti-malarial campaign interacted with the 'paternalistic vision' of RACM (Schumaker 2011: 420). The habitat of the mosquito was mapped onto the people associated with them. In this logic, these 'dangerous populations', for example Lamba traders in agricultural produce, were found in dangerous places, such as *dambos*, and pursued 'dangerous activities', such as brewing beer. These populations, places and activities had to be separated from the controlled environment of the corporate mine townships (Schumaker 2011: 416).

Corporate Towns

In his article on early urban development in Zambia, Gardiner (1970: 10) noted that 'Luanshya proved to be the prototype for the other "twin" towns established on the Copperbelt . . .'. 'Twin' referred to the corporate and government parts of the newly established towns next to the copper mines. However, there is more to the twofold character of these mining towns. A look at Luanshya's spatial arrangement reveals that the term 'twin' refers not only to administration but also to race (see Map 1.1). In retrospect, I consider three sets of practices crucial in the development of Luanshya's spatial order: town-planning schemes for mining sites from South Africa, the Garden City movement from Great Britain, and social welfare measures in order to be able to compete for mine labour with the Union Minière du Haut Katanga (UMHK) across the border in the Belgian Congo (now the province of Haut-Katanga in the Democratic Republic of the Congo).

Luanshya had started as a mine camp in the second half of the 1920s. Early on, both White and Black labour suffered from the poor living conditions in the camp, which had been racially segregated from the beginning. Spearpoint

(1953: 13) remembered how Europeans were accommodated in 'three-roomed buildings' and Africans in 'one-room huts'. The term for such a place, 'camp', and its internal division in the form of racial segregation based on the separation of different land uses called 'zoning' originated in the context of the South African mining industry.[13]

Labour accommodation and living conditions on the Copperbelt differed greatly from Windhoek, the Rand and Kimberly, where gold and diamonds were mined. The closed mine compounds that Gordon (1977: 29), Moodie (1994: 79) and Demissie (1998: 453) examined resembled prison camps, encapsulated by the outer walls of their dormitories around an inner courtyard optimizing surveillance to prevent theft (see also Leubuscher 1931: 61–64). In his reflections on 'camps', Agamben (1998: 169–70) drew attention to their 'paradoxical status' as 'a space of exception'. As the authors mentioned above have also shown in their work, mine camps were both an exception to the order around them and an integral part of the colonial enterprise. This ambiguity connected the Copperbelt mining towns with the camps in South Africa.

The spatial model of the 'camp' for the accommodation of male migrant labour on sites of mineral extraction in South Africa moved northwards and was observed in the 'total absence of privacy' within the compounds of Southern Rhodesian mines by van Onselen (1976: 35). Apart from the controls of access to mine townships noted by Parpart (1983: 45), the South African model was not reproduced on the Copperbelt. Thefts of copper involved larger quantities of ore and more elaborate logistics. Contrasting the 'camp', women 'had been induced to come [to the urban areas] by the Union Minière' (Higginson 1989: 69) in Katanga 'to improve health and social conditions' (Buell 1928: 562). Further to the northwest, labour at Companhia de Diamantes de Angola was accommodated not in mine compounds but in villages under the mine's administration (Cleveland 2015: 153). On a scale from the extremely restrictive and centralized model of the 'camp' in South Africa to the decentralized accommodation pursued in Portuguese Angola, mining towns like Luanshya started out as male migrant labour camps and gradually turned into mine townships for a very heterogeneous 'extractive community' (Larmer and Laterza 2017: 702). By 1931, Luanshya was recognized as a town (Smith 1985: 1490), and its segregated municipal townships started to develop. Corporate control over the mine townships was legally guaranteed by the 1932 Mine Township Ordinance (Parpart 1983: 39, footnote 48, 181).

Consequently, what Gardiner regarded as a core characteristic of Luanshya as a prototype and what Home (2013: 6) termed 'twin townships' referred to the separate company (mine) and government (municipal) parts of Luanshya *and* the respective European and African townships within them.[14] Map 1.1 (RACM 1951) illustrates this double twin composition: the European mine township around the park 'C', the 'R.A.C.M. African Township', the European government township 'L', and the African government township Mikomfwa, which was

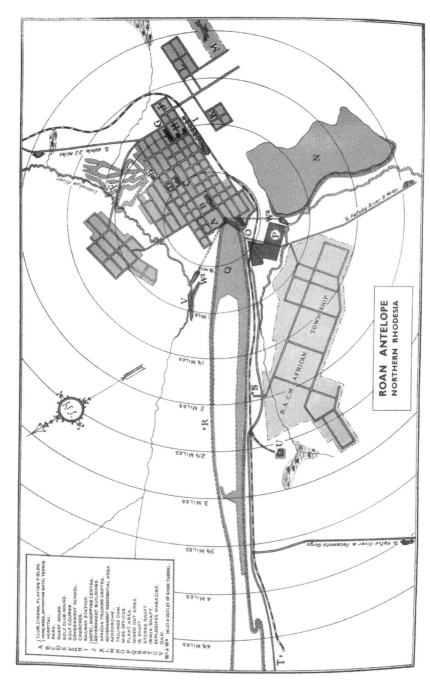

Map 1.1. Luanshya with its European and African mine and municipal townships, 1951. LSE Library Archives, London.

built south of the runway 'M' and east of the tailings dam 'N' from 1951 on-wards (Epstein 1958: 19).

Racial segregation became a cornerstone of the new spatial and social order on the Copperbelt, with '[the] segregated city not only [resulting] from but in many cases, [creating] the segregated society' (King 1980: 212). Looking at Map 1.1 once again, it can be seen that the Europeans lived in the low-density area at the heart of town further away from potential sites of industrial pollution. The Africans lived in a high-density satellite settlement, detached on the other side of the main plant 'P' and close to the shafts 'S' and 'T' along the ore body 'Q'. The contrast between the European and African living quarters on the Copperbelt was horrific. In a 1960 interview, Kenneth Kaunda, later the first president of independent Zambia, described it with reference to a mining town that could have been Luanshya:

> You travel along an avenue shaded by trees; on either side are the beau-tiful European houses with well-kept gardens where the garden 'boys' work. Under your feet is a good tarmac road. Suddenly the tar comes to an end, you are treading on a dusty red road. You have arrived in the African residential area. Now you see row upon row of huts and each is like the one next door. When the sun shines the hut becomes an oven, when the rain falls it becomes a well in the middle of a swamp. When it is cold the hut is like a refrigerator. How can a man and woman bring up their children decently in such surroundings? (Kaunda and Morris 1960: 41–42)

During my fieldwork in Mpatamatu, I revisited Kaunda's observation. On my way from downtown Luanshya to the township the roads changed from tar-mac to mud, the plot sizes decreased, and the houses became smaller. Homes felt like an oven during the dry season. Kaunda's observation was in stark contrast to how Watson remembered the European part of Luanshya from the days of the anti-malarial campaign. He wrote that RACM had constructed 'townships laid out like garden cities' (Watson 1953: 69). His association was certainly not related to Lamba understandings of *dambos* as subsistence gardens noted earlier, but to '. . . contemporary developments in British town-planning practice and garden city design' (Home 2015: 64). Particularly in the inter-war years, British town planners promoted the 'garden city' in the colonies, making colonialism a 'vehicle' of urban planning models (Home 2000: 330; King 1980: 206).

One of those town planners was Charles Compton Reade (1880–1933), who arrived in Northern Rhodesia in 1929 to prepare plans for Livingstone and Ndola (Home 1997: 157–63; Tregenza 1988). However, the ideals of the Garden City movement, aimed at combining British working-class neighbourhoods with the English countryside, could not be applied without conflict to the segregated mining settlements of Northern Rhodesia (Home 1997: 32; 2000: 343). In fact, the implementation of Garden City ideals in the colonial context was 'in sheer contrast to the original Howardian concept, essentially, ('anti-social' (Bigon 2013: 482). Reade negotiated unsuccessfully with the mines over general plans and eventually lost his job with the colonial government in 1932.

Home (1997: 32; 2013: 8, endnote 18, 21) suggested that Reade might have become a victim of the 'major conflict of philosophy' between the Garden City movement and the principles of segregation that were defended by the mining companies when he was found dead in a hotel room in Johannesburg in 1933. In following Schumaker (2011: 413), I can nevertheless discern the impact of the Garden City movement and its town-planning ideas on the corporate mining townships of companies like RACM. This influence came from the temporality of urban development on the Copperbelt, which started much later than in South Africa.

RACM awarded the planning of Mpatamatu to the South African town-planning consultants Collings and Schaerer. Major J.C. Collings and V.T. Schaerer had both been active in the Research Committee on Minimum Standards of Accommodation of the South African Council for Scientific and Industrial Research (CSIR), which was concerned with urban African housing. Collings had also been Director of Housing and a member of the National Housing and Planning Commission (South African CSIR 1947a, 1947b, 1948). This South African connection might explain the self-sustaining character of Mpatamatu as based on zoning and racial segregation. Mine township autarky was compatible with the company's goal of establishing a controlled environment that allowed supervision of the labour force. Elements of the Garden City movement found their way not only into the Copperbelt's European mine townships, but in one of 'the few cases' (Bigon 2013: 479) also into the spatial arrangement of African mine townships like Mpatamatu: tree-lined streets and garden-like playgrounds in section 21 (see Map 1.2; RACM 1957, drawing number NR.RA2), with a park belt separating sections 22 and 23 (see Map 0.1).

The location and time for the construction of Mpatamatu were related to the position of the copper ore underground, movements in the copper price and labour tensions in the 1950s. Luanshya had started as a mine camp on the south-eastern tip of the ore body. Racial segregation and shaft development along the ore body towards the northwest resulted in the first African mine township of Roan being constructed opposite the Storke shaft ('S' in Map 1.1). When the mine reached the Irwin and MacLaren shafts further west, opened in 1948 and 1963 respectively (Coleman 1971: 10–11; Cunningham 1981: 165), and more labour needed to be accommodated in close proximity, Mpatamatu was born as RACM's second African township in 1957. Roan was considered too crowded

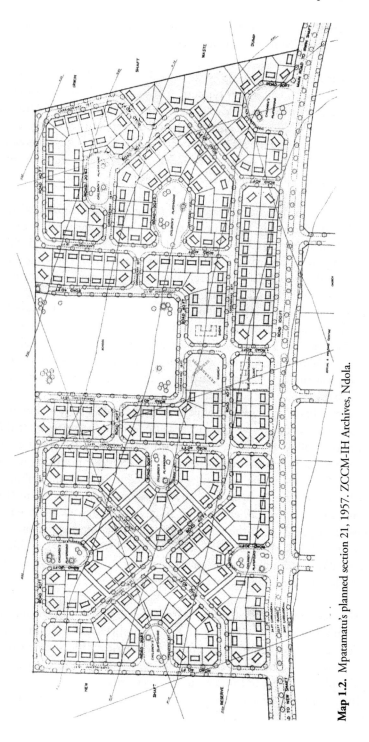

Map 1.2. Mpatamatu's planned section 21, 1957. ZCCM-IH Archives, Ndola.

and distant from the newly developed shafts.[15] A study of the social services in Mpatamatu for RACM management noted:

> Mpatamatu African township is to be built because the movement of mining westwards will otherwise cause many employees to live too great a distance from their work; . . . It is also said that transport of Africans by rail to Irwin and MacLaren Shafts will interfere increasingly with the surface ore transport system and with cage schedules. It is therefore intended eventually to house all or nearly all the mining departments' African labour in Mpatamatu. (RACM 1960b: 2)

The copper price had been steadily increasing since the Second World War (*Horizon* 1965). The war in Korea drove the price still higher until it reached an all-time peak in 1955/1956 (*Horizon* 1959a; Roberts 1982: 348, 355–57). The high price of copper caused its replacement by aluminium, bringing the price down at the end of the 1950s. Prices remained relatively stable in the 1960s and early 1970s (Cunningham 1981: 173). This was a rare condition in a market characterized by inelastic supply and demand, both being relatively insensitive to changes in price. Subsequent over- and underproduction usually resulted in price volatility (Stürmer 2009: 19–20). The market situation in the 1950s and 1960s made mine development and the extension of production feasible. As a result, Mpatamatu was built on the congruent growth of copper supply and demand against the backdrop of the Cold War.

However, Mpatamatu was not built as an integrated mine township with extensive corporate welfare provisions just because technicalities necessitated it and the copper price allowed it. After the Copperbelt strikes in 1935 and 1940, the conflict over African unionization increased in the 1950s, culminating in another strike in 1956.[16] The mining companies attempted to counter the politicization of the labour force through paternalistic provisions of social welfare (Parpart 1983: 140–43). As noted earlier, working and living conditions had been crucial in Luanshya's early days in the competition for skilled and experienced mine labour with UMHK (Higginson 1989: 94; Parpart 1983: 34–35). Collings and Schaerer's 1957 development plan for Mpatamatu substantiated the corporate characteristics of the new mine township accordingly:

> 1. The new township, extending westwards from Irwin Shaft and on the southern side of Irwin Shaft and the New [MacLaren] Shaft, is intended to accommodate 3,584 houses for married African employees. The houses are to be single detached units and the prescribed size of a regular plot is 50 feet in frontage and 70 feet deep.
> 2. The planning must allow division of the residential areas into sections, each section to be in association with its administrative offices, welfare

buildings, etc., and each section to have its own water reticulation and electrical systems. Ten sections of 358 houses each are suggested.

3. Provision must be made for Schools, Welfare Halls [i.e. social clubs], Clinics, Sports Fields, Cinema, Beer Halls, Parks, Churches, Trading Sites, and Market, Administration Offices, First Aid Station and Maintenance Workshops. (RACM 1957: II)

The mining companies owned and controlled everything within the mine townships of the Copperbelt. RACM and all its successors prior to the reprivatization of the sector in 1997 – Roan Selection Trust (RST), Roan Consolidated Mines (RCM) and Zambia Consolidated Copper Mines (ZCCM)[17] – were responsible for the construction and maintenance of Mpatamatu's infrastructures in the form of roads, houses, electricity, water and sewerage. They provided all basic communal services, namely health care, leisure and adult education (primary and secondary education was largely outsourced to the colonial and later national government). The three paragraphs from Collings and Schaerer's plan quoted above summarize my earlier elaborations on the location and time for the construction of Mpatamatu. The township was to serve the extraction of the ore underground and provide social amenities for its mineworker residents and their dependants. Paragraphs two and three in particular qualify Mpatamatu as what Crawford (1995: 5) termed a '"new" company town'.

Mine labour accommodation on the Copperbelt was related to models not only from other parts of southern Africa but also North America. Crawford, who explicitly included mining towns in her work on the design of company towns, set out from the premise that they represent a 'regulatory mechanism' aimed at controlling the labour force and countering labour unrest. She identified elements of the Garden City movement in the design of the '"new" company towns' in North America: the decentralization of communities, the linking of industrial and agricultural activities, and beautifying urban areas with tree- and grass-lined streets (Crawford 1995: 6–7, 70–75, 151). These characteristics appeared in Mpatamatu's detached location near a mine shaft, its division into sections, the presence of subsistence gardening alongside industrial labour (*Horizon* 1968: 32–33; Perrings 1979: 24), and the spatial design proposed by Collings and Schaerer.

The construction of Mpatamatu started with sections 21 and 22 in 1958 (see Map 1.2 and Figure 1.1; *Horizon* 1965: 24). According to a handwritten note on the draft pages of a 1960 social services study, the first houses were occupied in November 1959 (RACM 1960b: 6). Sections 23 and 24 followed in the first half of the 1960s (see Figure 1.2; *Horizon* 1968: back cover). These four sections became the new home for mineworkers working at the Irwin (now the 18th) and MacLaren (now the 28th) shafts (RACM 1960b: 3). Section 26 was developed in the first half of the 1970s, sections 25 and 27 eventually in the second half of

Figure 1.1. Mpatamatu's section 22 under construction, late 1950s. LSE Library Archives, London.

the 1970s. These three western sections were occupied by mineworkers of Baluba shaft, opened in 1972 (RCM Luanshya Division 1972).

Mpatamatu was continuously developed over a period of approximately twenty years from the late 1950s to the late 1970s. In total, the township comprised 4,701 residential units and fifty 'commercial, recreational, other' buildings according to a municipal valuation roll in preparation for the mine's reprivatization in 1991 (LMC 1991).

Its construction history was recalled by many of its residents. Most of the information I acquired through interviews corresponded to archival records. Several research participants remembered when the different sections were constructed or whether their family was the first to occupy a mine house. Moreover, they recalled the housing contractors: Amlew, Costain, Delkins, Ford, Morta and Roberts. Roberts from South Africa built houses in sections 22 and 24.[18] Costain, a British construction company, erected the houses in section 23.[19] Morta from Zambia was involved with the construction of section 25, and Amlew, the building and civil engineering division of Anglo American, with section 27 (Charter Consolidated Limited International Appointments Division 1970; RCM Luanshya Division 1974).

A look at Map 0.1 reveals the substantial differences between the older (eastern) and newer (western) sections of Mpatamatu. Sections 21 to 24 were developed under the principles outlined in Collings and Schaerer's 1957 development

Figure 1.2. Mpatamatu's section 23, 1964. ZCCM-IH Archives, Ndola.

plan: hierarchized roads, alternating house directions, changing street layouts, playgrounds and social welfare buildings – in short, features that made each section a 'small socially self-contained residential unit' (RACM 1957: 6) marked by Garden City movement conceptions. This is despite the fact that, for instance, section 22 underwent additional densification (RST Roan Antelope Division 1962b).

In contrast, sections 25 to 27 showed few of these features. Construction was based instead on the principle that as many mineworker families as possible should be housed. This is mirrored in their housing densities. While sections 21 to 24 have an average of 576 houses, sections 25 to 27 have 798 houses each on average.[20] The rather spartan layout of the more recent sections had its roots in the strained economic situation and budgetary limitations of the 1970s, as summarized by the Roan Mpatamatu Mine Township Management Board (RMMTMB):

> Finally, 1973 has been a year of the ups and down for Zambia and therefore Mpatamatu Township being a small part of Zambia is no exception. (RMMTMB 1974b: 5)

Mpatamatu thus became the last extension of Luanshya as a mining town. The township was special because it represented an elaborately and comprehensively planned mine township for the African labour force. Unlike Roan township, Mpatamatu did not grow out of the first living quarters that made up the mine camp in the early days of RACM (RST Roan Antelope Division 1964f). No grass-thatched rondavels were erected for African mineworkers in Mpatamatu (*Horizon* 1959b: 6). The township was not occasionally supplemented to meet corporate, government or labour requirements. It was developed and erected in accordance with concrete corporate provisions, the social welfare buildings at the core of this book.

Corporate Provisions

At the heart of Mpatamatu and the corporate provisions for its residents rested the social welfare buildings, infrastructure that the former chairman of RST Ronald Prain (1907–1991) summarized as 'amenities' that included 'hospitals, clinics [and] welfare centres' (Prain 1956: 309). The term 'welfare' is ambiguous in this context. In the first place, these buildings were not meant as charitable institutions for the labour force. They were not the materialized Polanyian 'counter-movement' initiated by the colonial government in order to 'check the action of the market relative to labor, land, and money' (Polanyi 2001: 136, 79).

Rather, these 'amenities' were sites of corporate action to control the work-force in the face of a decline in labour turnover and an increase in unionization. As Parpart (1983: 152) noted, '[welfare] services aimed to divert miners from more controversial organisations' (see also Luchembe 1982: 390). Beer halls, clubs and sports facilities kept mineworkers occupied after work. Mine clinics monitored the labour force's health. Community centres integrated women into the mine's labour regime and defined their role as housewives responsible for the social reproduction of the labour force. These buildings represented a separate in-frastructure that was capable of '[bending] human routines and material practices to its will' (Howe et al. 2016: 551).

Extending from the Foucauldian notion of power translated into built envi-ronment in Demissie's (1998: 454), Home's (2000: 327) and Njoh's (2009: 302) abstractions of mineworkers' housing in southern Africa, I understand Mpata-matu's social welfare buildings as an example of corporate paternalism and as fundamental aspects of the mine's disciplinary architecture setting the boundar-ies for social life. They provided for 'the controlled insertion of bodies into the machinery of production and the adjustment of phenomena of population to economic processes' (Foucault 1998: 140–41). The social welfare buildings estab-lished what Epstein termed the '"unitary" structure of the mine':

> It is important to bear in mind what I may term the 'unitary' structure of the mine. As I have already explained, the mine is a self-contained indus-trial, residential, and administrative unit. Every employee is housed by the mine, and no African who is a mine employee may live off the mine premises. Moreover, until recently, every African was fed by the Com-pany, and the vast majority of the employees continue to draw weekly rations from the Company's Feeding Store. A butchery and a number of other stores enable those who wish to supplement their rations to do so without making a trip to town or the Second Class Trading Area. It is the mine which provides the hospital, and employs the doctors and nurses who care for the sick; and it is the mine, again, which provides for the recreational needs of its employees. The African miner writes his letters at the Mine Welfare Centre, he drinks with his friends at the sub-Beer Hall on the mine, he prays in the church of his own denomination on mine property, he sends his children to school on the mine. In the work situation he has an allotted place within the structure of the mine. He has a job within a department, works together with the members of his gang under an African boss boy, who is in turn responsible to a European supervisor, and so on. In short, the mine impinges on his life at every point, a state of affairs which is epitomized in the office of the African Personnel Manager [C.F. Spearpoint at that time], who is ulti-

mately responsible for almost all matters arising within the African Mine Township. (Epstein 1958: 123–24)

This '"unitary" structure of the mine' was an example of institutionalized corporate paternalism. The labour force was 'cared for' through central provisions by the mining company. This 'care' was based on 'strategies of inclusion and exclusion' (Schlee 2008: 35–42) within the 'fatherly' (Latin *paternus*) relationship of the company, in the form of its management, with its workers and their dependants.[21] This fatherly relationship was epitomized by the infantilizing language of White compound managers like C.F. Spearpoint in Luanshya (Spearpoint 1937). Integration in respect of this relationship was characterized by an 'interplay of difference and sameness' (Schlee 2018: 14–15). Corporate paternalism appealed to a shared identity, that is, to being employed by, part of and dependent on the mine. Management and labour force belonged to the same unit and were thus part of the same 'body' (Latin *corpus*), in other words, the 'corporation' (Schlee 2018: 6). At the same time, this unit was hierarchically structured on the inside, most prominently in the form of the colour bar. This politico-corporate order and its socio-economic consequences based on difference excluded the largest part of the predominantly African workforce from decision making.

As Epstein showed, belonging to the mine worked both through inclusion, for example through infrastructure such as the social welfare buildings, and exclusion, for example the hierarchy structuring the labour regime and the administration of the mine township. Sameness and difference penetrated people's lives at the mines in what Schlee (2008: 5–11) termed 'modes of integration'. As I show in the next section on corporate abandonment, the integrative potential of the mining companies decreased after ZCCM's privatization. This was particularly the case in Mpatamatu, where the mine retreated from its social investment. This abandonment turned integration based on selective corporate sameness into a nostalgic image of a paternalist past with lost opportunity.

Much of Epstein's observation and analysis can be related to Goffman's concept of the 'total institution'. This concept combined the three aspects of life that Goffman (1990: xiii, 5–6) saw in 'sleep, play and work' under a single authority. Despite the fact that Goffman's typology of total institutions included 'work camps' and that Davies (1989) refined the concept, the ethnographic context of its development was not productive workers in company towns but the inmates of mental hospitals. Moodie (1994: 88) pointed to this fact, and Goffman (1990: 21) himself drew attention to the incompatibility between total institutions and the 'work-payment' environments of social life. In contrast, Hughes (2010: 4) claimed that the 'company town [was] another excellent example of a total institution', while Porteous (1972: 63) called the company town 'a total environment'. Following Moodie in departing from a Goffmanian abstraction of the mining compounds, Sparks (2012: 173) showed how corporate paternalism was 'co-produced' at Suid-Afrikaanse Steenkool, Olie en Gaskorporasie or the South African Coal, Oil and Gas Corporation (SASOL).

In light of these reflections on the explanatory range of Goffman's 'total institution', I return to Epstein's (1958: 123–24) observations, which stemmed from the same field site as my own ethnographic data. The term 'unitary', in my view, also emphasizes the institutional character of the mine in general and the social welfare buildings in particular. It attributes these social provisions to the company while retaining enough conceptual space for the everyday practices of a company town's residents, who at times challenged the order they lived in. In this sense, I suggest that the concept of the 'total institution' obstructs appreciation of residents' agency. This aspect was important in the context of Luanshya in how township residents and the larger extractive community made and continue to make a living.

Thus, the social welfare buildings shaped township life in Mpatamatu. Table 1.1 at the end of this chapter provides an overview of them. The buildings were nodal points in a network through which power worked and '[weaved] itself into . . . everyday practices' (Luthar and Pušnik 2010: 10), material representations of Foucauldian 'governmentality'.[22] Collings and Schaerer's development plan for Mpatamatu made it clear that the mine was engaged in what Devisch (1998: 225) termed 'social engineering', that is, the interplay between shaping the material environment and moulding social life under corporate colonialism. The 'landscape [was] part of the operation of power' (Cane 2019: 3) and unfolded in what Casid (2011: 98) termed 'the performative, landscaping . . . the interrelations of humans . . . and what we call the "environment"'.

The unitary structure of the mine in Luanshya remained intact after Zambian independence in 1964 and the nationalization of the copper sector in 1969/1970. This continuity is my reason for employing the term 'corporate paternalism' to characterize the mine's presence and corporate practices in Mpatamatu up until the copper sector's reprivatization in 1997. At the same time, I refrain from using the term 'corporate social responsibility' (CSR) in the context of post-reprivatization Mpatamatu because 'old regimes of corporate paternalism [were not] reinvented' (Rajak 2011: 10; see also Dolan and Rajak 2016: 6) in the township. My research participants repeatedly juxtaposed the corporate absence of CNMC Luanshya Copper Mines (CLM) in Mpatamatu with the continuous provision of opportunities provided by the mine in the township before 1997.

In following Ferguson (2006: 197), I wanted to mark the colonial roots of the mine townships: the provision of worker housing, the maintenance of recreational facilities, the subsidies distributed in kind. I saw the civilizing mission of the colonial era being translated into the corporate care of the mining companies and their modernist ideas on what progress meant for their labour force. In contrast to other structural changes in Zambia's copper industry, such as the dismantling of the dual wage structure and the replacement of expatriate workers in a process of 'Zambianization' (Burawoy 1972a; Sklar 1975: 110–11), I argue that the paternalist social project persisted in the mines' relationship to their labour force until the 1990s. This condition changed selectively with the advent of neoliberal reforms in Zambia propagated by the Bretton Woods institutions. In Luanshya, CSR practices by CLM were mapped onto existing practices of spatial segregation, only affecting the permanent labour force. Consequently, and in contrast to Luanshya city centre, Mpatamatu and its residents were left behind by the successors of corporate paternalism.

Corporate Abandonment

The involvement of the World Bank and the International Monetary Fund (IMF) in Zambia's copper sector constituted the background to one of the most fundamental transitions in the lives of most Copperbelt residents. In his article on Zambian reactions to neoliberal reform, Larmer (2005) identified one particular outcome of structural changes within Zambia's copper sector that I argue were closely related to the post-privatization situation in mine townships like Mpatamatu. Neither the creation of the parastatal ZCCM advised by the World Bank in 1982 nor its dismantling enforced by the very same institution in 1997 had the effect of increasing investments in Zambia's most important industry. Instead, the foundation of ZCCM resulted in substantial outflows from the sector to the ruling United National Independence Party (UNIP), while ZCCM's privatization resulted in mines like that in Luanshya 'being asset-stripped' (Larmer 2005: 34–35). Even worse, the structural readjustments did not shield production from a low copper price or mineworkers from being laid off.

ZCCM's privatization resulted in a gradual retreat of mining operators from the mine townships, their infrastructures and residents' lives.[23] Mine houses were sold to their tenants, typically in a transaction involving a deduction from the terminal benefits that mineworkers received from ZCCM. The corporate abandonment of the industry's social investment resembled the change that had been described in the Lusophone context during decolonization as a 'process of emptying out' (P. Gupta 2015: 181). Mine employees and township residents lost access to welfare facilities because the buildings were no longer considered part of the mine. The buildings in turn lost the people who regularly visited them because departments responsible for them were dissolved and mineworkers were retrenched.

In a neoliberal reorientation, mining companies refocused on the mines as sites of mineral extraction. The presence of the mining industry on Zambia's Copperbelt went from, in Ferguson's (2006: 35–36) terms, 'socially thick' to 'socially thin'. Before 1997, mineworkers had been 'incorporated into a social system' and, as will also become evident in the following chapters, 'paternalistic relations of dependence were . . . central to workers' identities' (Ferguson 2013: 227, 228). Building on Larmer's work (2005) and a Rights and Accountability in Development (RAID 2000) report, Gewald and Soeters came to the following conclusion in their in-depth study of the reprivatization of Luanshya's mine:

> Through the relentless pursuit of profit for investment capital, the liberalization and privatization of the mines has led to the destruction of the social structure of the mines, not only in Luanshya/Baluba but more generally. (Gewald and Soeters 2010: 165)

Luanshya deserved particular attention in this process of 'the destruction of the social structure of the mines' for several reasons. First, ZCCM's Luanshya Division, one of the oldest Copperbelt mines with an extensive welfare infrastructure, was the first asset to be sold to an outside investor in October 1997. Second, the transaction was overshadowed by the fact that ZCCM's Privatization Negotiation Team (PNT) abruptly reversed its decision to accept the offer of First Quantum Minerals (FQM). Instead, it awarded the contract to Binani Industries, a company that had not conducted any underground studies at the mine, was inexperienced in copper mining, and that specialized in scrap metal. Binani Industries' profile and the sudden change in awarding the contract aroused widespread suspicion (RAID 2000: 162–65). The head of the PNT Francis Kaunda (not related to Kenneth Kaunda) later tried to diffuse this suspicion by publishing his own account of ZCCM's privatization (Kaunda 2002: 42–57). Nevertheless, he was sentenced to jail in connection with certain irregularities during the restructuring of Zambia's copper sector in 2008 (Donge 2009: 79, 88; *Lusaka Times* 2008). Third, the 'development agreements' that legalized the transfer of the parastatal's divisions from public into private management did not safeguard the sustainability of the social services at each mine.

Civil unrest and strike action spread on the Copperbelt in October and November 1998. Mpatamatu was the scene of these protests, culminating in fights with the local mine police forces (RAID 2000: 154, 184). According to the agreement settling the sale of ZCCM's Luanshya Division, Binani Industries' subsidiary Roan Antelope Copper Mines of Zambia (RAMCOZ) assumed control of and responsibility for the social services related to the mine. The respective paragraph reads:

> The company has assumed ownership, operational control and responsibility for the social assets connected to the mine. These comprise the medical and educational services (two hospitals, nine clinics, and one trust school), recreational facilities, sports clubs and essential municipal infrastructure, including electricity and water supply and sewerage systems. The company agrees to apply existing eligibility criteria for registering dependants entitled to these services. (RAID 2000: 188, based on Clifford Chance 1997: 17–20)

The RAID (2000: 188–89) report stressed that there were several clauses in the agreement that enabled the mining company to retreat from its social obligations in the mine townships without the government being obliged to step in. RAMCOZ was permitted to contract out the management of social facilities. This process had already started in Mpatamatu in 1985, when ZCCM (1985) leased out the township taverns to private individuals. The abandonment of the mine's social structure proceeded under RAMCOZ from 1997 to 2000 and the subsequent private and government receivership. Moreover, within three years Binani Industries' subsidiary had piled up a mountain of debt that the government receivership was still struggling to neutralize at the time of my fieldwork.[24] The value of former social welfare buildings was repeatedly assessed in order to sell them and get them out of the receivership's portfolio.[25] When the mine was reopened by Luanshya Copper Mines (LCM) in 2003, most of the mine's social assets remained in receivership with RAMCOZ.

At the time of my fieldwork, two facilities in Mpatamatu, the pay line buildings and the section 23 clinic, were formally run by CLM. The introduction of salary transactions under RAMCOZ had already rendered the pay line buildings useless for CLM's predecessors. The section 23 clinic was being run as the last remaining mine clinic in Mpatamatu. The separation of 'core' mining and 'non-core' social assets (RAMCOZ (in receivership) 2001) and the World Bank-financed transition of mine townships into municipal entities (World Bank 2000) resulted in a dramatic redefinition of Mpatamatu: it was no longer a mine township with little involvement by the government, but a municipal township full of abandoned corporate remains with insufficient involvement by the government. By the turn of the millennium, the '"unitary" structure of the mine' (Epstein 1958: 123–24) had ceased to exist:

> ZCCM provided almost everything that held society together in the Copperbelt: jobs, hospitals, schools, housing, and a wide range of social services including HIV-AIDS and malaria awareness and prevention programmes. Towards the end of the ZCCM era, much of this effort was collapsing. The new investors have made little effort to pick up these responsibilities. They are clear that their 'core business' is mining, and that the provision of social infrastructure goes beyond this remit. According to free-market ideology, and the Development Agreements, these goods and services should now be provided either by the local authorities or by market forces. (Fraser and Lungu 2007: 4)

The retreat of RAMCOZ and its successors, LCM and CLM, from the mineworkers' living quarters in Mpatamatu took away a variety of opportunities that had been based on the mine's corporate provisions. Endemic undercapitalization was the main economic condition following the mass retrenchments in the early

2000s,[26] making the takeover of the former social welfare buildings by outside companies or individuals highly likely. The privatization of the buildings that did not remain with the mine was set to follow the same pattern as the privatization of ZCCM: dismantling, sale to outsiders, asset reassessment, depreciation and uncertainty over new investments.

In Mpatamatu, one building, the former section 21 housing office, was sold to a commercial actor from outside. Bayport Financial Services, a Mauritian financial service provider, first rented and later acquired the building where mineworkers and their dependants were previously allocated mine houses. Until the closure of Baluba underground mine in September 2015, the branch office in Mpatamatu was run to offer micro-finance solutions such as loans, deposits and money transfers. It has been placed under maintenance since then.[27]

All the other former social welfare buildings that were abandoned by the mine were taken over by stakeholders previously linked to the township through their residence or workplace. Despite, or rather because of this fact, the process of privatizing the 'non-core social assets' meandered through ZCCM lease agreements, rental contracts issued by RAMCOZ, sale advertisements, letters of offer, and partial payments to the receivers. The buildings existed in a state of 'suspension' (A. Gupta 2015), a separate temporal state between corporate abandonment and legal privatization. Consequently, the statuses of owner and tenant became blurred over time. Sitting tenants found themselves in a relatively strong position vis-à-vis the receivership and potential investors from outside. They organized themselves in the RAMCOZ Social Assets Sitting Tenants Association, which had repeated successes in making its voice heard at State House in Lusaka (Manchishi 2013; Musonda 2014).

Ruination after Paternalism

Processes of disintegration accompanied me throughout my fieldwork in Mpatamatu. They touched every house in the township and people's everyday lives. The conditions overwhelmed me from time to time. I passed through kitchens with electric stoves being used as shelves while food was being prepared on *imbaula* braziers using charcoal outside. I used bathrooms equipped with a ceiling lamp, shower and flush toilet while being instructed to use a torch and water in a bucket procured from a well. I looked up to the street lights that once illuminated the township's most important arteries while experiencing the complete darkness of night in Mpatamatu.

Residents talked a lot about material deterioration. However, in conversations about the former social welfare buildings, their material conditions were left to one side, and the loss of social opportunity became the focus. Like the buildings, our exchanges cross-cut the material–social divide. Research participants illustrated what the material infrastructures in the township and their deterioration meant for social life in Mpatamatu. I came to understand this change in residents' living conditions through Stoler's concept of 'ruination' (Stoler 2008b). I recognized it as a productive conceptual analogue to what I had observed and recorded, and to what I had learned from the public discourse on the corporate paternalism of the past. In a Zambian commentary online on 'what Zambia has lost', I read that '[it] is an embarrassing fact that any mining town in 1957 or 1977 had better maintained social welfare and youth facilities than in 2017' (Mulenga 2017). This was exactly the cross-temporal perspective that I encountered when I interviewed residents of Mpatamatu.

'Ruination' allowed me to focus on the 'corrosive process' taking place at the former social welfare buildings, locations that had been abandoned by their corporate creators. The concept reached into the past and grasped imperial continuities which persisted up to the time of my fieldwork. It considered the 'material and social afterlife of structures, sensibilities and things' (Stoler 2008b: 194), providing a tool with which to trace the material in the social and vice versa from the past to the present. Finally, 'ruination' focused 'not on inert remains but on their vital refiguration' (Stoler 2008b: 194), speaking to my observation that people in Mpatamatu creatively reappropriated what had been left by the mine.

Stoler (2008b: 194) developed the concept based on the literature on 'ruins', Benjamin's (2002) *Arcades Project* in particular. She refined the concept, originally designed for a material site, to one identifying a socio-material process (see also Mah 2008: 16–17). Simmel (1958: 379–85) had provided the starting point for Gordillo (2014: 9–10), who positioned 'rubble' against 'ruin' in order to tear down the latter's glamorized ascriptions. He 'interrogate[d] ruins as objects in which space, history, decay, and memory coalesce' and that triggered memories and transplanted past living conditions (Gordillo 2014: 2, 256), a capacity I also observed in Mpatamatu. Other scholars had used Benjamin and Simmel's reflections as a basis for the way they thought about ruins producing politics (Dawdy 2010: 777), dialectical disharmony (Boym 2011) and culture (Göbel 2015: 135–70).

In my view, the literature shared the mapping of material corrosiveness onto the concepts of the 'ruin' and 'ruination'. I acknowledge that the reappropriations I was interested in were intertwined with concrete sites of material decay. Howe et al. (2016: 552) emphasized how ruins, or broken infrastructure, rendered themselves visible by becoming 'acute', thus exposing social conditions. For Edensor (2005a: 842), ruins were at 'an intersection of the visible and invisible'. In this sense, the remains of Mpatamatu's social welfare buildings made the invisible loss of opportunity visible.

Stoler amalgamated the site and the process, the visible and the invisible, the ruin as a 'byproduct of capitalism' (Schwenkel 2013: 257) and a 'snapshot of time and space within a longer process of ruination' (Mah 2008: 16). She proposed that 'we might turn to ruins as epicentres [of creative human action]' (Stoler 2008b: 198). However, in their reappropriation of the former social welfare buildings, people were *creative*, something I missed in the semantics of the concept of 'ruination'. Was 'ruination' still the determining process of their innovative actions? Mpatamatu took me to the conceptual edges of 'ruination' and, ultimately, left me with the question of what came after it.

Table 1.1. Mpatamatu's former social welfare buildings.

No.	Building	Owner	Main tenant	Main use	Page(s)
1	Buseko Recreation Club	RAMCOZ in receivership	Club committee	Bar	87–88, 92, 97
2	Kabulangeti Community Centre	RAMCOZ in receivership	MPACE	College	58, 79–80
3	Kabulangeti Tavern	RAMCOZ in receivership	Private	Church	101–104
4	Kalulu Recreation Club	RAMCOZ in receivership	Private	Bar	92–93
5	Kansengu Community Centre	RAMCOZ in receivership	Private	Vacant	56, 78–79
6	Kansengu Library	ZESCO	ZESCO	Service	78
7	Kansengu Tavern	RAMCOZ in receivership	Private	Bar	90–91
8	Kansumbi Tavern	RAMCOZ in receivership	Private	Bar	91
9	Mpatamatu Pay Line	CLM	Suzika Private School	School	42, 55, 76–77
10	Mpatamatu Stadium	RAMCOZ in receivership	Mpatamatu United FC	Stadium	93–98
11	Mpatamatu Sports Complex	RAMCOZ in receivership	PAOG(Z)	Church	96–98, 104–106
12	Muliashi Community Centre	RAMCOZ in receivership	Golden Eagle Private School	School	59–60, 80–81
13	Mwaiseni Tavern	RAMCOZ in receivership	Private	Bar	91–92
14	Section 21 clinic	RAMCOZ in receivership	Serve Zambia Foundation	Administration	105
15	Section 21 housing office	Bayport Financial Services	Bayport Financial Services	Service	43
16	Section 23 clinic	CLM	CLM	Clinic	42
17	Section 25 canteen	RAMCOZ in receivership	Private	Bar	92
18	Section 25 clinic	Ministry of Health	Ministry of Health	Clinic	66, 81
19	Section 26 clinic	Ministry of Health	Ministry of Health	Clinic	69

At this point, I would like to conclude by situating Mpatamatu as a scene of ruination and renovation for the subsequent chapters. The township was built as a corporate project in direct relation to the extraction of copper at a mine that owed its existence to corporate colonialism. It was integrated into a segregationist order within the mining town of Luanshya on the Central African Copperbelt. Mpatamatu's corporate infrastructures, particularly its social welfare provisions, established it as a company town. However, the paternalistic order ruling the mine township collapsed after Zambia's copper sector was reprivatized. Abandoned by the mine, corporate remains in the township decayed while at the same time being reappropriated for different motives: from reviving a paternalistic vision and starting a business to providing meeting places for Mpatamatu's population.

Notes

1. See Gann (1964: 63), Home (2015: 56), Krishnamurthy (1969: 588), Larmer (2005: 43), Roberts (1976: 192).
2. See Bradley (1952: 28–39), Luchembe (1982: 57–58), Perrings (1979: 6), Siegel (1989: 2).
3. For sources on this expedition and a biography of Collier, see Bradley (1952: 64–74).
4. Sheldon Daniel Chanda, interview with the author, 29 March 2016, Luanshya.
5. On the role of 'scientific' prospecting techniques in the development of the Copperbelt, see Frederiksen (2013), Luchembe (1982: 196).
6. See Bradley (1952: 97), Gann (1964: 209), Letcher (1932: 163), Luchembe (1982: 131).
7. See Phillips (2009: 220–4), Selection Trust (Undated), *The Times* (1968).
8. Rajak (2011: 66) noted that 'foundational myths are important then, not only in the construction of corporate identity, but in naturalising the company's position in the broader historical landscape of industrial capitalism in South Africa'.
9. Based on Spearpoint (1953: 15). On Spearpoint's career at RACM, see *Horizon* (1960).
10. See Waters (2019) and Chansa (2020) for recent studies of epistemological claims in environmental knowledge put forward by the mining industry.
11. Based on Coetzee (1953: 149).
12. See Chauncey (1981: 138–51), Eccles (1946: 8), Siegel (1988: 77).
13. See Englund (2002: 140), Gardiner (1970: 10), Macmillan (2012: 539).
14. On the case of Nkana in Kitwe, see Mutale (2004).
15. See the 'Locality Plan for Construction Sites' in RST Roan Antelope Division (1964b).
16. See Branigan (1956), Forster (1940), Parpart (1983: 54–95), Russell (1935).
17. On the mine's corporate history, see Faber (1971b: 22), Potter (1971: 111), RACM (1961b), Republic of Zambia (1982), Roberts (1982: 348–49).
18. RST Roan Antelope Division (1962a, 1964c). Roberts was started by Douglas Roberts (1906–1982) in 1934. The company changed its name to Murray and Roberts in 1974 and was listed as Masimba Group at the time of my research. See Bruce (2012), Masimba Group (2013).
19. RACM (1961a), RST Roan Antelope Division (1962a). Costain was started by Richard Costain (1839–1902) in 1865 and profited substantially from infrastructure projects within the British Empire. See Costain Group (2015), Njoh (2009: 305).
20. Calculations by the author based on LMC (1991).

21. See also Sparks (2012: 21, 186) on the case of the South African Coal, Oil and Gas Corporation (SASOL).
22. On the explanatory power of Foucault's concept in the context of Copperbelt, see Frederiksen (2014).
23. On ZCCM's privatization process, see Craig (1999, 2001).
24. Administrator General and Official Receiver of RAMCOZ, interview with the author, 17 May 2016, Lusaka.
25. See Grant Thornton (2004), RAMCOZ (in receivership) (2001, 2004, 2013).
26. Richard Kafunda, a former Zambia Consumer Buying Corporation store manager, explained to me how 'undercapitalization' was the main economic problem caused by the retrenchments following RAMCOZ's bankruptcy. The retail sector did not collapse but was downgraded to a level of low-cost products. Richard Kafunda, interview with the author, 12 May 2016, Mpatamatu.
27. Bayport Financial Services Luanshya Office Staff, interview with author, 5 May 2016, Luanshya.

Chapter 2

Of Men and Women

'*Muzungu! Muzungu!*' These shouts welcomed me as I stepped onto the veranda of a house in the western part of Mpatamatu's section 26. Its structure set it apart from the standardized former mine houses around it. The building had been a store from which mineworkers' wives used to buy their groceries. The owner closed it down in the course of the economic recession in the early 2000s following the mine's reprivatization in 1997. He started to rent out the premises to a private school, one of many that mushroomed in former corporate and private buildings within the township. It was around noon and the pupils were heading home, passing me with shouts and laughter. Some were mimicking what they thought was spoken Mandarin in the belief I was one of the Chinese who had been working at the mine since its takeover by CNMC Luanshya Copper Mines (CLM) in 2009. Apparently, the first association of a stranger in this part of Zambia was in the process of moving from a European *muzungu* to a Han Chinese.

The founder of the private school, a former government primary school-teacher resident in Mpatamatu since 1970, was waiting for me in one corner of the large room. I entered what must have been the sales area in the past. The room was divided by cupboards to provide separate areas for different classes. Tables, chairs and letter pictures gracing the walls diverted my attention from the material state of the building to its practical reappropriation as a school. Born in 1949 in Eastern Province, the woman had followed her husband when he came to Mpatamatu. He took a job at the mine when the entire sector was nationalized in 1969/1970. Apart from her secondary education in the town of Chipata in the late 1960s, she had mostly lived in rural areas. She had arrived in Mpatamatu like many other women as an immediate dependant of her husband. Asked about her move to a mine township like Mpatamatu in the first place, she recalled: 'I was impressed. The life I had to live was very different'.[1]

In conversation, the woman teacher remembered distinct material experiences that marked her arrival and new life in a mine township. While she used to sleep on a reed mat in a thatched hut, a bed and sheets awaited her in her brick house, which was covered with asbestos roofing provided by the mine. Subsistence farming ceased to be the economic basis of the household she was supposed to head. Instead, she spent a share of her husband's salary at grocery stores like the one formerly accommodated in the building in which we were talking. A 1970 photo feature 'Progress is Contrast' in Roan Antelope Copper Mines' (RACM) corporate *Horizon* magazine exalted the various forms of infrastructure people gained access to by settling in a mine township like Mpatamatu based on the material differences between 'backward' rural and 'modern' urban life (*Horizon* 1970a: 10–17).

Corporate paternalism was based on a gender division of labour that attributed household management and the social reproduction of the workforce to women. Initially, the mining companies and the colonial government wanted to uphold the dependence of women on men in order to retain indirect rule through the chiefly authorities (Parpart 1986a: 144). However, women had always challenged, altered and replaced this dependence on men. When I conducted fieldwork in Mpatamatu, the township represented not a miners' place based on a male social order, but rather a collection of infrastructural remains that challenged both men and women equally. The township had endured the privatization of Zambia Consolidated Copper Mines (ZCCM) and its neglect by successive mine operators. However, women's socio-economic position had changed in the face of these transitions in Mpatamatu.

In this chapter, I investigate the changes in the relationship between men and women before and after the industry's reprivatization. I do so by looking at the position of particular material locations in Mpatamatu within this relationship, namely the former pay line buildings and community centres. My starting point is the 'stabilization of labour', that is, the decrease in the turnover of labour, a process described by managers and scholars alike as becoming established with the development of the copper industry.[2] Home (2000) showed how this stabilization was made possible by changes in the industry's accommodation for its labour force in the 1930s. It marked the beginning of the large-scale settlement of women and children in the Copperbelt's mine townships, a development which had already taken place at Union Minière du Haut Katanga (UMHK) across the border in the Belgian Congo (Higginson 1989: 61–85).

I retrace women's different practices to both accommodate and challenge their position as dependent housewives under RACM and the Roan Selection Trust (RST) through secondary literature. Based on my own fieldwork, I follow women to homecraft classes, women's clubs and formal mine employment at the community centres under Roan Consolidated Mines (RCM) and ZCCM's Luanshya Division. Finally, I revisit the post-privatization mass retrenchments of the early 2000s, which mainly affected the men, and the ever-growing economic importance of women in township households.

All aspects of this chapter are connected by the extension of my ethnographic observations into the past and my enquiry into the role of Mpatamatu's former social welfare buildings in the relationship between men and women. The programmes at the community centres showed me that women have always been of socio-economic importance to mineworkers' families. Women were central to the organization of women in the township in what I argue was a maternalist extension of corporate paternalism. Women countered the sharp decline in male wage labour after the privatization of ZCCM by taking up employment themselves and by extending previous economic activities. Unlike most of their husbands, who were used to working full-time at the mine, these women had consistently pursued agricultural subsistence work alongside running a household. This chore provided a vital backup in times of high unemployment and was the entry point for a general reorientation in Mpatamatu away from the modernist vision of urban consumerism towards self-sufficient livelihoods rooted in agricultural subsistence.

Accommodating Women

Established patterns of labour migration existed in southern Africa when RACM opened a recruitment office in Fort Jameson (now Chipata) in 1928. In general, men from the rural areas in the north-eastern part of southern Africa went to the mines in Katanga, Southern Rhodesia and South Africa.[3] The Copperbelt became a new destination within these existing patterns. The majority of its mineworkers turned out to be Bemba-speaking peoples from Northern Province (now Northern and Muchinga Provinces). This was also the case in Luanshya (Mitchell 1954: 8; RST Roan Antelope Division 1968). The shift from a temporary migratory to a permanently resident labour force was only made possible by the increased presence of women and children in the mine townships, which necessitated other forms of accommodation and additional infrastructures.

While in 1941 the colonial government had 'showed itself unwilling to commit itself to the policy of establishing a permanent industrialized native population on the Copperbelt' (Hailey 1950: 146–47), the 1948 Urban African Housing Ordinance pressed the mining companies to provide accommodation for employees *and* their dependants (Home 2000: 341). The 1952 Ordinance on Urban African Housing underlined this requirement for every employer in urban areas, the mining companies being the most important of them (Unsworth 1957: 3). When Mpatamatu was started in 1957, family housing was an established

Figure 2.1. A 'category 5A' mine house from Mpatamatu's section 23. Photo by the author.

corporate provision on the Copperbelt. The majority of the 4,700 residential units constructed in Mpatamatu were of 'category 5A'. The houses comprised three rooms, each being introduced to accommodate a mineworker and his family (see Figure 2.1).[4]

However, the mines realized that accommodating women was not enough to ensure their cooperation in the industrial complex. In the early 1930s, RACM had reacted to the influx of women by providing agricultural plots for subsistence vegetable farming. This was a first step in a process that integrated women into the company's African mine township and its larger economy. As Chauncey (1981: 139) noted, there was both a social and an economic rationale for absorbing female labour. Women produced food rations at a lower cost than outside professional farmers. The highly gendered urban integration of women went back to female practices in rural areas, such as sowing, harvesting, cooking, brewing and fetching water (Richards 1969: 382). In that sense, female labour in the mine townships represented one of the many links that connected the mines and their townships to distant rural life when it came to everyday practice.

Rural Urbanity

How rural/agricultural and new urban/industrial areas were related to each other through migration has been an academic topic since the first collection of essays on the Copperbelt's industry edited by Davis (1967) in 1933. Subsequent research carried out by the Rhodes-Livingstone Institute (RLI) followed up on this theme (Mitchell 1951; Wilson 1941, 1942). The topic re-emerged at the centre of a debate on the 'historiography of transition on the Zambian Copperbelt' in the 1990s. Ferguson (1990a, 1990b, 1994) accused the RLI of conducting research under a modernist bias and of ignoring the significance of rural–urban ties for people's lives in the mine townships. He criticized any attempt to periodize social adaptation to life at the mines and questioned the ability of the concept of 'stabilization' to grasp the complexity of social practices that cut across the rural–urban divide.

Following Macmillan's (1993, 1996) reactions to Ferguson, I neither perceive the RLI's analysis of social change and urbanization as 'modernist' or as misjudging the adverse consequences of urbanization for the rural social order, nor do I regard their research as being ignorant of the significance of rural–urban relations for people living at the mines. Rather, Ferguson (1990b: 618) misrepresented the RLI's research when he reproduced Gluckman's famous dictum that 'an African miner is a miner, an African townsman is a townsman' and concluded that, for Gluckman, urban residents' 'rural pasts were of little significance to the analysis of their urban behaviour'. In fact, the opposite was the case.

Gluckman (1956: 17) noted the 'significant' influence of a miner's or townsman's origin on his behaviour on the very same page as the quote above.[5] Mitchell had worked with the concept of 'stabilization' to correlate the decrease in African labour turnover with the increase in Africans taking up urban residence. His typology of people living in the Copperbelt's mining towns did not at all neglect rural links. He cautioned that 'attitude' – that is, the tendency to go about one's life with a particular set of social practices – should be derived from the duration of urban residence (Mitchell 1951: 23–27; 1954: 15).

'Rural pasts' surfaced in my everyday fieldwork. Mineworkers turned into farmers, formerly dependent housewives into agricultural self-supporters. Rural pasts pervaded the literature on the history of Luanshya as an industrial site. Schumaker (2008: 832) pointed to the former agricultural use of *dambos* (see Chapter 1), while Epstein (1958: 230) showed how tribal representation dissolved into labour-based unionization. It is important to reiterate Peša's (2020: 544) contention that, irrespective of the employment situation, agricultural subsistence production always coexisted alongside formal industrial wage labour in the urban centres of the Copperbelt, not only during strikes (Parpart 1986b: 48; Powdermaker 1962: 124). I frequently crossed over from Mpatamatu's eastern to its western part through the Nkulumashiba *dambo*, which was covered with maize fields and vegetable gardens. I realized the presence of urban industrial pasts, such as the abandoned headgears of the 28th and 18th shafts on the horizon, the pot-holed tarmacked streets and the former social welfare buildings that stood out from the increasingly agricultural present of Mpatamatu.

The tension between the township's urban spatial arrangement, in the forms of the sections, streets and aligned houses, and its practical appropriation, that is, the makeshift shops, houses-turned-businesses and random farm plots, induced me to look at Mpatamatu from the perspective of 'space [as] a practiced place' (de Certeau 1988: 117). It was above all what de Certeau (1988: 91–93) termed 'texturology', or the materialized representation of a particular planning vision, that accorded Mpatamatu its urban character. The township had been the mine's '"own" place', created in a hegemonic way. This place was challenged by a 'space of tactic' in which those who inhabited the place used and subverted it. These 'tactics' accommodated the spatial order in which people lived according to their needs (de Certeau 1988: 35–37; Crang 2011: 108).

Gluckman (2006: 16) saw the behaviour of African labour migrants as rooted in 'social situations'. It was influenced by migrants' rural origins and their urban residence, but above all by the situation itself (Gluckman 1956: 17; Werbner 1984: 161). Parpart (1986a: 147–52) found that women in RACM's first African township Roan were housewives, brewers, gardeners, petty traders, housekeepers, gamblers, prostitutes and mine employees. Clearly, these activities were influenced by the corporate living environment at the mine. Women continually adapted themselves to the changing face of the mine townships and the facilities provided by the mining company within them.

In Mpatamatu, Luanshya's second and, in comparison to Roan, more comprehensively planned African mine township, more material corporate provisions marked the 'social situations'. They ascribed social positions to men and women in their relationship with each other. During my fieldwork, I saw how women were turned into housewives and employed by the mine. At the former community centres, female domesticity was institutionalized by employing women in social welfare programmes. Some women started to instruct other women on how to be 'modern' housewives. These programmes were based on the corporate and government view that women needed to be occupied. The 1938 *Pim Report* had called for more welfare measures for women:

> Some welfare work has been carried out by the mines and it is now being extended by the appointment of welfare sisters, financed in equal shares by the mines, by Government and from beer hall funds. Other proposals for expenditure from beer hall funds include libraries and swimming baths. *There is a great deal of leeway to be made up in these directions, especially in providing new interests and occupations for the large number of women* [emphasis added]. (Pim 1938: 47)

Occupying Women

Educational and economic programmes organized at Mpatamatu's community centres became the corporate practice to provide 'new interests and occupations' for women. The programmes were a direct consequence of the increased presence of women that was a result of labour stabilization. Women programmes were a paternalistic practice that was also rooted in an attempt by the mine to 'divert miners away from politics and towards social and economic advancement' (Parpart 1983: 141). Similarly, miners' wives were supposed to strive for the social and economic advancement of their families. The mining companies were convinced that to this end women of rural origin had to be instructed on how to lead 'modern' urban lives. Clearly the change in the material living environment was substantial, as the teacher at the beginning of this chapter confirmed. In Luanshya, RST actively encouraged mineworkers to send their wives to the community centres. Its *Citizen Handbook* for Roan and Mpatamatu mine townships from the early 1960s read:

> At other centres, your wife can learn how to run a modern home. Classes are held in needlework, cookery, child welfare, hygiene and homecrafts. (RST Roan Antelope Division Undated: 13)

These 'other centres' were in fact community centres or 'women centres' that had been started in Mindolo, a township of Kitwe, in 1939. The idea for the centres originated in the 'educational and welfare work' of the United Missions in the Copper Belt (UMCB), a collaboration of several missions (Parpart 1986a: 146; Taylor and Lehmann 1961: 39, 45). The centres became a material representation of the three Cs that had been propagated by David Livingstone (1813–1873): Christianity, commerce and civilization. The mining companies welcomed European missions as a disciplining force into their townships. Plots in Mpatamatu had been reserved for church buildings from an early stage in the township's development (RACM 1960a: 3; RST Roan Antelope Division 1963a). Taylor and Lehmann (1961: 34, 45) noted that sometimes prayer houses were built by the mining companies themselves and that UMCB's European women volunteers were found on the welfare committees of each mine on the Copperbelt by 1945. The (European) African Women's Welfare Officer in Roan writing about turning 'African wives' into 'help-mate[s]' like in any other 'civilised community' in *Horizon* magazine (Lloyd 1960: 27), the content of the classes mentioned in the *Citizen Handbook* above and the women in white aprons at one of Roan's women centres listening to the welfare officer Boniface Koloko (*Horizon* 1963: 20) all illustrate McClintock's assessment that 'African women were subjected to the civilizing mission of cotton and soap'. The gender division of labour on the mines reverberated with what she termed the 'gendering of imperialism' (McClintock 1995: 31; see also Evans 2015).

The classes at the community centres extended corporate paternalism from the male workers to their female dependants. Men had been linked to the company through their work down the shafts. Women entered into a direct relationship with the mine through the programmes at the community centres. African men had been turned into 'boys' by their White superiors. Being infantilized became a social experience at the mines both under and above ground. Accordingly, women became 'modern housewives' by making them students of the industry's modernism, a corporate practice that survived political independence (Ferguson 1999: 166–67). As noted by McClintock, to 'civilize' the African population had been an imperial practice under British colonialism. In 1957, a welfare supervisor wrote to the African personnel manager at Rhokana (now Mopani Copper Mines (MCM)) in Kitwe:

> By changing [African women's] norms and educating them to appreciate the necessity for health, hygiene, family discipline, and a rigid adherence to moral codes, and the rewards to be had from honest endeavor and self-help, we will aid them in developing a new culture, which, based on our ideology and concepts of Christianity and democracy, will be within their concepts of tribal social life and therefore understood and acceptable to them. (Cited in Parpart 1986a: 147)

The fact that mineworker husbands were instructed to send their wives to homecraft classes revealed the male order underlying the social relations between men and women in the mine township. Mining was for men and of men: their labour represented the basis of the entire industry. The household was for women: they were responsible for the social reproduction of the male workforce. This division, between men in formal employment and women in formal dependence, made men the breadwinners of mineworker families. Men's employment opened up the paternalistic provisions of the mine that cemented their dominant socio-economic position. Former mineworkers' wives told me how they *only* needed their husbands' mine IDs to visit a clinic, collect food rations or shop in the township's grocery stores and have items delivered to their homes. Allocations were subject to employment, and women subject to their husbands in receiving them.

The position of the social welfare buildings within the relationship of men and women revealed two ways in which women were dependent on men to make a living in a mine township like Mpatamatu. Legally, women needed their husbands' identity as mine employees to gain access to the 'amenities' of the township and the provisions made available to them. Financially, women needed a share of their husbands' salary to run the household. This need increased when the mining companies abolished food rations and introduced inclusive wages in the mid-1950s (Parpart 1986a: 153).

Women handled these dependencies in various ways. Chauncey (1981: 145, 150) found that some women generated their own income, most efficiently by brewing beer. Others became 'responsible for managing the family budget'. Harries-Jones (1964: 44) documented how women fought for their 'proper supply of food and clothes' at the mine's advice bureaus. Mpatamatu's residents told me how women followed their husbands to the pay line buildings on pay day in order to secure their share of their husbands' incomes immediately. Others took a job at the mine as nurses, teachers or typists.[6] Mijere's (1985: 300) survey showed that some women who had joined the classes at the community centres eventually ended up trading, a biographical trajectory that I also found in the lives of my research participants.

The biography of Fenia Muyutu, a former social worker at the community centres in Roan and Mpatamatu, illustrates how the socio-economic position of women in a mine township changed from being dependent on men and regulated by the company to being employed by the company, provided with economic opportunities and equipped with business skills, which proved crucial after the fall of corporate paternalism. Born in 1959 into a mineworker's family, Fenia Muyutu had first gone to school in Luanshya's Roan mine township before giving birth to her first child at the age of sixteen. A home economics course at a Catholic mission opened the door for her to later become a homecraft teacher and youth organizer. In 1978, she was employed by RCM and was allocated a single-quarters house like unmarried men. During her time at the mine, she rose to the G5 supervisor pay grade (see endnote 13). After her marriage in 1982, she moved with her husband when he was transferred to ZCCM's Luanshya Division in 1983.[7]

On a tour of Mpatamatu's three former community centres, Fenia Muyutu recalled the details of corporate programmes for women. At Kansengu Community Centre in section 21, Mpatamatu's oldest centre built in the early 1960s (RST Roan Antelope Division 1962a), she explained to me what her job as a homecraft teacher had comprised: 'We were teaching them housekeeping, budgeting, child care and sewing, and gardening'.[8] Courses were organized over a duration of six months and were usually attended by fifteen to twenty-five women.[9] She taught on a daily basis in the mornings and afternoons. Classes were mainly for women, but they were also offered to girls. Gardening courses were open to boys, too (RCM Luanshya Division 1977). Kansengu Community Centre also housed Mpatamatu's advice bureau, the same corporate institution for domestic dispute management that Harries-Jones (1964) had investigated in neighbouring Roan township.

Standing in front of her former classroom with me, Fenia Muyutu directed my attention to the room next door, which once housed a kitchen with two electric stoves. The idea of cooking with electric appliances in the township seemed completely removed from Mpatamatu's reality and almost sceptical to me. Long power cuts were the rule during my fieldwork. The electric stove turned into a symbol of a past filled with modernist 'expectations of domesticity' (Ferguson 1999: 166–206). In contrast, the *imbaula* brazier told of the township's immediate economic conditions: it was made from scrap metal, needed no electricity, and ran on charcoal, a fuel that was locally produced and cheaply available, albeit with devastating consequences for the local environment (Peša 2017).

The homecraft classes for women had started as a corporate attempt to control women and to dictate how they were supposed to navigate the urban living environment. The classes followed the same paternalist logic that had first incorporated men into the industrial complex. Inspired by Lankton's (1991: 163) reflections on how Lake Superior copper mines 'nurtured a man's body, mind, and soul', I see this functional nature of Foucauldian 'biopolitics' and its use to relegate bodies to their prescribed positions (Foucault 1998: 140–41) also being at work in Luanshya.

RACM recruited men, transported them to the mine, provided accommodation and food rations, subordinated them to the racist labour regime and the work underground, and allowed them to be regenerated at the mine hospitals and leisure facilities. Similarly, women were accommodated as housewives, sent to garden plots, educated at community centres, and taken care of at the mine section clinics. Women's mere presence in the township drew them into the mine's 'political field' (Foucault 1995: 25–26), one shaped by the power relations connecting the African and European labour forces, their dependants and the company with each other.

However, looking at the paternalistic provisions of the mine in Luanshya from the perspective of a functional understanding of 'biopolitics' falls short of the conceptual capacity of Foucault's reflections on power, potentially resulting in an analytical bias towards the imperial formations that created the Copperbelt's spatial order and mine townships like Mpatamatu (see Chapter 1). The different occupations of women in the township revealed how the apparent straightforwardness of a spatial urban design was dissolved into the complexity of everyday social practice. Collier (2009) emphasizes that Foucault in fact gave a 'topological' nature to 'biopolitics'. At its core is a correlation of different 'technologies of power'. 'Biopolitics' must be understood as a 'problem space', an analytical space that examines the diverse practices of power without reducing material sites and social phenomena to any one prevailing source of power (Collier 2009: 79, 88–89, 93).

The economic and educational programmes at the community centres had been part of RACM's and RST's corporate strategy of defining the position for women. After independence, the gendered division of labour at the mines remained in place. To this day, mine labour is dominated by men with few exceptions (Musonda 2020). 'Zambianization', the replacement of skilled expatriate workers with Zambian personnel, was all about men (Burawoy 1972a). The state-owned successors, RCM and ZCCM, continued the programmes for women at the community centres, sustaining the homecraft teacher as another female job category. The centres remained focused on the education of women and girls as housewives. However, women's clubs in particular fostered joint economic action and solidarity networks among women.

Figure 2.2. Former Kabulangeti Community Centre in section 24. Photo by the author.

Kabulangeti Community Centre in section 24 opened in 1963 (see Figure 2.2, RST Roan Antelope Division 1963c). Fenia Muyutu explained to me how different women's clubs engaged in poultry-breeding and tailoring. She pointed down Kamilendo Street (see Map 0.1), where the mine had provided a building to serve as a chicken run. The clubs did not have to pay any rent and shared the profits from selling the meat. Other women were sewing baby dresses, which were directly distributed to new-born infants at Roan's mine hospital. Payment for their work came from the mine. The clubs represented a fusion of earlier attempts by the mining company to take advantage of female labour and women's initiatives to generate their own income in order to reduce their dependence on men.

Infrastructure once provided for women, emblematic of the unitary structure of the mine extending its authority over women, was hard for me to imagine as we walked down the pot-holed Kamilendo Street towards the southern boundary of the township. A concrete rubbish dump with traces of ash surrounded by dried-up maize plants was all Fenia Muyutu and I found in the place where chickens were formerly raised to be sold in the township's market. Poultry-breeding still existed in Mpatamatu, but it had moved from corporate infrastructure spanning community centres, women's clubs and other mine facilities to the back gardens of the privatized mine houses. Mine township autarky, once outlined for Mpatamatu in the 1957 development plan, had been reduced to private autarky.

From being forced to circumvent the highly regulated order of the mine township, often resorting to practices prosecuted by company and tribal representatives, women entered the homecraft classes as students and teachers like Fenia Muyutu. African women took over these classes and the organization of women from European women volunteers. Hartnack (2016) investigated the role of European women in the education of African women and their reproduction as housewives under colonialism in the context of Southern Rhodesian farms. He identified a crucial correspondent to the paternalism underlying the gendered organization of labour, which he referred to as 'domestic maternalism'. Inspired by mission schools, White 'farmers' wives' played 'the role of the nurturing mother-figure to the resident [Black] population' (Hartnack 2016: 49–54, 62–67). This role was played out in homecraft clubs for women on the farms.

Similarly, I see 'domestic maternalism' represented by the homecraft classes and the women's clubs run and organized at the community centres in Mpatamatu. However, in following Hartnack's (2016: 66) reference to Law (2011), I do not understand the homecraft classes and women's clubs in mere functional terms, placed exclusively in the service of the company to 'civilize' and 'modernize' mineworkers' wives. African women became their own teachers, like Ada Phiri featured in the *Horizon* (1963: 20) article on Boniface Koloko mentioned above, or Fenia Muyutu at the Kansengu Community Centre. Women organized themselves into micro-cooperatives at the Kabulangeti Community Centre, while others like Fenia Muyutu became nursery and pre-school teachers at the Muliashi Community Centre. Moreover, women eventually used the skills acquired at the community centres to make a living outside the mine economy.

Fenia Muyutu remembered her time as a pre-school teacher at Muliashi Community Centre (see Figure 2.3). She was posted to the two small shelters next to the main building in 1984. The centre had become operational in the second half of the 1970s.[10] Next to the characteristic C-shaped main building[11] were a playground, a netball court and a football pitch. Fenia Muyutu prepared children aged five to six for school by teaching them reading and writing. Her classes usually ran for up to three hours in the mornings. The chairs piled into one of the shelters still hinted at that particular past.

Fenia Muyutu and myself entered the main building from the back through a passageway and stopped in front of the western wing. The toilets had been abandoned and become dysfunctional. The main building stood in silence: red brick walls, grey concrete tiles, eroded asbestos roofing and gaping broken windows

Figure 2.3. Former Muliashi Community Centre in section 26. Photo by the author.

behind bars. Occasionally, the doors to the run-down toilets would bang against the wall because of a weak breeze in the September heat. The green around the centre, which I remembered from my first visit in April 2016, right after the rainy season, had given way to a dusty ochre. Abandoned playground equipment was the only thing pointing to the usual presence of the pupils of a private school, who had left for the holidays (see Chapter 3).

Rather than leaving women to fend for themselves outside corporate control, the provision of 'new interests and occupations' (Pim 1938: 47), such as home-craft classes and women's clubs, integrated women into the unitary structure of the mine as both participants and instructors. The centres were corporate places that enabled the company to extend its bodily control over women and children. In return, the women took advantage of the educational and economic programmes for their own personal ends. The community centres both reproduced women as mineworkers' housewives and opened up paths for women to increase their economic self-reliance.

After being retrenched from ZCCM in 1986, Fenia Muyutu first turned to cattle-trading. In the early 1990s, she ran a chicken business from her private home. At the time of my fieldwork, she grew maize for her family plus a small surplus to be sold in the market. Her economic activity had been marked by what Mususa described as the 'villagisation' of life in Luanshya.[12] To Mususa, villagisation was the approach of 'thinking about place regardless of how it is *politically* categorised (urban or rural), [focusing] much more on what a place affords its inhabitants, and the affective experiences it generates' (Mususa 2014: 38).

Informal economic activities, prominent in Luanshya since the early 2000s, have been conceptualized by Mususa (2010: 385) through the concept of 'trying'. From one's social life being set by mine employment, it became 'a journey of attempts and improvisations' (Mususa 2014: 104). 'Trying' was rooted in a Gluckmanian situational negotiation between people's own agency and the structural conditions in the townships. From the perspective of Fenia Muyutu's biography, two main characteristics of 'trying' were evident. First, privatized mine houses became the centres of economic activity. Second, agricultural subsistence practices moved from the margins to the centre of household economies (see also Mususa 2010: 384; 2014: 97). The industry's idea of the 'modern' consumerist home had become an urban past.

Retrenching Men

How dramatically the respective positions of men and women had changed since the privatization of ZCCM's Luanshya Division can be illustrated by looking at the experiences of two couples whom I interviewed and spent time with on several occasions. The husbands' lives provided vivid examples of how personal biographies were moulded by the history of the mine in general and the township of Mpatamatu and its social welfare buildings in particular. Their biographies are interspersed with material experiences made in those buildings. Both men were born into mineworker families in the early 1960s. Their fathers worked in RST's Luanshya Division, the successor to RACM. Their families were among the first to take up residence in the newly developed township of Mpatamatu at the turn of the 1960s. One of the two had been born at the township's first mine clinic in section 21, which opened in 1959 (Federation of Rhodesia and Nyasaland Ministry of Health–Northern Rhodesia 1959). The other went to pre-school at Kabulangeti Community Centre. They both went to the government primary schools in the township, engaged in after-school activities at the community centres and visited secondary schools in neighbouring Roan township. Eventually they became mineworkers themselves, both starting out as general workers at the lowest employment levels G6 and 7 under ZCCM in 1985 and 1990 respectively.[13]

The dismantling of ZCCM marked a turning point in each man's life. Being born into mineworker families, their lives had always been connected to the material living environment run by the mine: the clinics, the community centres, the sports facilities, that is, the social welfare buildings erected exclusively for mineworkers and their dependants. Binani Industries' asset-stripping through RAMCOZ and the bankruptcy of the subsidiary that ensued marked the beginning of a process of social and material ruination. The men were not only retrenched, ruining their economic and social lives, they also lost access to the mine's corporate provisions. The social welfare buildings were ignored by subsequent mine operators, ruining the landscape in which the men and their families lived. One of these two men managed to get re-employed by the mine in 2010 after several years of trying as a businessman. In 2014, he was discharged permanently by CLM's subcontractor, China 15th Metallurgical Construction Group Corporation (15MCC).

There are two issues in the lives of these men that I would like to emphasize. First, a look at one of the men's payslips reveals the extensive nature of a husband's position as the family's breadwinner. Second, retracing the other man's participation in training programmes in order to accommodate technical changes in the industry exemplified the active approach of some men to the task of saving themselves from unemployment in an increasingly mechanized industrial sector.

RCM and ZCCM continued the corporate paternalism first introduced by the private enterprises that had run the mine from before independence until the industry's nationalization in 1969/1970. Corporate paternalism included what many Zambians consider the economic favouritism towards mine employees that led scholars to identify the mines' workforce as a 'labour aristocracy' (see Chapter 3). The nature of this subsidization becomes clear from looking at the 1992 ZCCM pay statement in Figure 2.4. Earnings in the right-hand column listed basic pay, production bonuses, allowances based on the pay scale and job per-

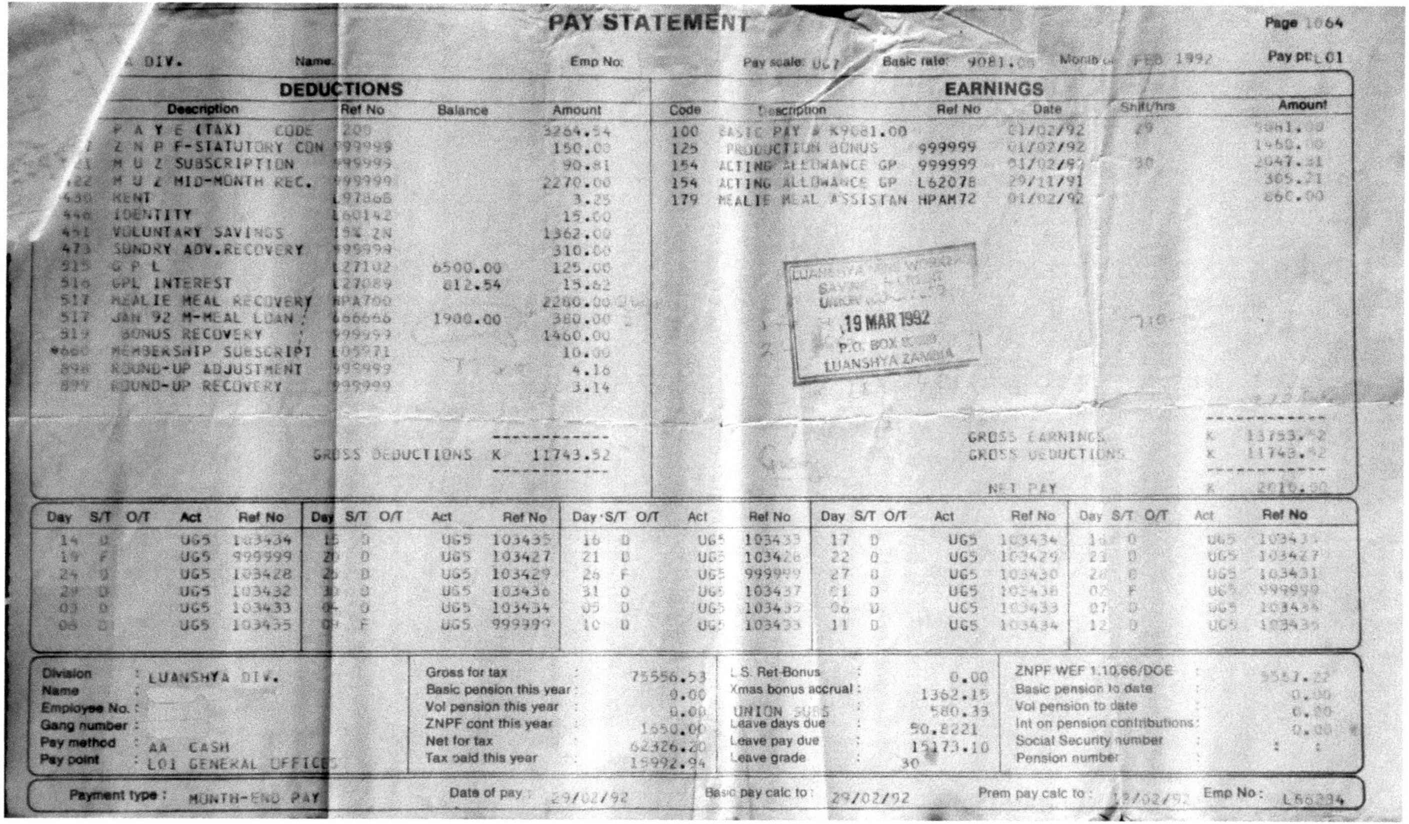

Figure 2.4. ZCCM payslip of an underground miner, 1992. Document courtesy of resident of Mpatamatu.

formed, as well as a mealie meal allowance.[14] In the case of this particular underground mineworker of the lowest level, UG7, the acting allowance acknowledged his work in the capacity of a worker two tiers up at the level of UG5.

The deductions in the left-hand column included income tax (PAYE, i.e. pay as you earn), the Zambia National Provident Fund (ZNPF) pension scheme and the Mineworkers Union of Zambia (MUZ) subscription fee. These general deductions were followed by positions special to the mines: a subsidized rent for the mine house being occupied, a voluntary savings scheme, a loan scheme and additional subsidized mealie meal. One fifty-kilogram bag was complimentary; above that, bags were deducted from the salary and accounted for on the payslip. The 'employee number' pointed to the paternalist provisions not accounted for by the figures on the payslip. Mine houses were provided with free water, sewerage and electricity (including the bulbs). Groceries could be bought at subsidized rates on credit and delivered to one's home, for example essentials such as cooking oil, eggs and meat. Mineworkers' children were eligible for free nappies and education allowances. Health care for a mineworker's family was organized through the employment number, usually referred to as the 'mine ID', at the section clinics of the township. The husband's job at the mine provided an all-round economic basis for mineworkers' families and women's domestic labour as housewives.

My second case follows a mineworker's attempt to accommodate himself to the changes in the mining industry by acquiring new qualifications. Samuel Yumba joined ZCCM to work at the Baluba underground mine in 1985 and began as a G7 general worker. A threshold on the path to job advancement was the blasting licence he acquired in 1992. A promotion to a G4 supervisor for earth-moving machine operators underground followed the year after. Moving earth underground inspired him to learn how to do it on the surface, and he joined a training course to become a dumper-truck driver. After his exit from and re-entry into the mine, Samuel Yumba was employed as a driver during the development of the Muliashi open-cast mine. CLM had taken over the mine in Luanshya from Luanshya Copper Mines (LCM) in 2009 with only the Baluba shaft in operation. According to former mineworkers, the 18th and 28th shafts had remained flooded since RAMCOZ's bankruptcy. During the time of my fieldwork, CLM placed Baluba into maintenance. Muliashi pit became the single site of extraction in Luanshya and the cornerstone in the transition from underground to surface mining of the ore body. As a driver who had helped clear the bush, Samuel Yumba became aware of this transition and went on another training course that would make him eligible for the roles of supervisor and instructor for drilling operations on the surface as a 15MCC employee.[15]

Samuel Yumba's initiative was in stark contrast to the local discourse on mineworkers as forsaken victims of the industry lost in the wasteful spending of their terminal benefits and the consumption of alcohol. I did encounter men with such derailed biographies and witnessed widespread alcoholism in Mpatamatu, but this is in no way representative of the full range of social trajectories set in motion by the mine's reprivatization. Unfortunately, all the qualifications Samuel Yumba acquired did not prevent him from being retrenched. Subcontractors' work in open pits was organized by season. Emulating the ticket system of the colonial days of the Copperbelt's mines, mineworkers like him had to lurch from one contract to the next. Furthermore, twenty-five years of work at the mines had taken their toll on his health. Finally, 15MCC failed to renew his contract in 2014. He returned to his house and plot, which he had bought from his terminal benefits in 1997. Behind the house, he showed me his self-made chicken run and the vegetables growing there. 'The only hope we have is going into the bush', remarked Laurence Banda, another former mineworker who had served for over twenty years.[16] While Laurence Banda was referring to the fact that people like him were literally going into the bush outside the township to farm, I observed people like Samuel Yumba bringing 'the bush' into Mpatamatu in their back gardens.

The transition whereby 'the bush' comes into the township clearly contradicts previous ideas about an urban Copperbelt, home of the industry, and its rural hinterlands, home of the labour force. While early RLI research on urbanization by Wilson (1941, 1942) had stressed the rural–urban dichotomy, follow-up research by members of the Manchester School adopted a more integrative stance by looking at rural and urban areas as part of a single sphere subdued by capital (Kapferer 2006: 150). I therefore support Mususa (2014: 48) in her view that the dichotomy is analytically useless when describing social change in post-reprivatization mining towns like Luanshya.

The research participants in my fieldwork have simply been trying to make the best of particular situations for themselves and their families. For many this involves agricultural activities in their back gardens, on undeveloped land in the township and in 'the bush' south of Mpatamatu. At the core, these situations are linked by post-industrial ruination: the decline of formal employment, the decay of infrastructures previously related to this formal employment, and a restructuring of household economies away from men towards women.

Replacing Men

After the reprivatization of Luanshya's mine, women's labour became crucial for their families. The former government teacher in the initial vignette at the beginning of this chapter did not retire but founded her own school to generate an income for the household. Fenia Muyutu had been a mine employee herself. From the social work for women at the community centres of Roan and Mpatamatu in the service of the mine, she went into livestock trading and ultimately subsistence agriculture. She had to replace her retrenched husband's salary. The wives of the two former mineworkers presented above followed a similar trajectory. They started as housewives dependent on their husbands and cared for by the mine, before stepping in and generating the main source of income for their families.

Both women were born in the 1970s, one into a family in Zambia's Southern Province, the other into a mineworker's family living in Mpatamatu. While the latter received her education at the township's schools and had lived there ever since, the former came to Luanshya through a relative in pursuit of tertiary education in 1991. Upon getting married, the women moved in with their husbands. Both knew what it meant to live the life of a housewife able to use the mine's infrastructures through her husband's identity as a mineworker. They gave birth to children in Roan's mine hospital and sought health care at Mpatamatu's section clinics. These living conditions changed in the wake of their husbands' foreseeable unemployment in the early 2000s. One woman joined a teachers' college and returned with a primary schoolteacher's certificate in 1999, while the other headed for a service company related to the mine. They managed to get into formal employment in 2000 and 2008 respectively.

Ruination in Mpatamatu was experienced by men and women as a retrenchment, a loss of status, exclusion from corporate provisions and exposure to material decay. These experiences multiplied with the number of dependants in a mineworker's household. The housewife-turned-teacher introduced above provided the sole income for her family at the time of my fieldwork. She was the only person in formal employment among her nine siblings. She and her husband had taken in three children of deceased relatives and accommodated the family of their first grandchild. They had all lost access to the mine's provisions and all depended on the woman's salary as a primary school teacher, an income from the government payment of which was frequently delayed. Asked how the family managed to make a living, the woman replied: 'Well, here and there'.

In terms of their contribution to the household, women moved from domestic work and casual earnings to increased economic activity and formal employment. They replaced men as breadwinners not only because the ending of corporate paternalism removed men's central socio-economic position, but also because women themselves took the initiative, leaving their positions as formally prescribed 'dependants'. Families in Mpatamatu explained to me how formal employment decreased mainly for men after the mine's reprivatization. The majority of retrenched workers in the early 2000s were men. Many of them went into the informal sector, previously a domain of women. According to a survey by Smart (2014: 267), the share of households participating in urban agriculture in Luanshya rose to 93 per cent.

The situation for some women moved in precisely the opposite direction. Thus, Samuel Yumba's wife joined a security firm subcontracted by CLM. The looting of mine equipment and metal infrastructure components had surged after RAMCOZ had started dismantling mine facilities for scrap metal in front of everyone's eyes. To protect the mine's property remained a huge challenge for every mine operator. Sometimes the security companies themselves were in-volved in the thefts (Wangwe 2016). As if to complete the total reversal of the positions of men and women in Mpatamatu, Samuel Yumba's family was eligible to visit the last remaining mine clinic in the township and the mine hospital in Luanshya through his wife's employment. It was *her* ID that *he* needed to receive treatment. However, the state of corporate health facilities had deteriorated after ZCCM's privatization (Tembo 2009: 77). Mpatamatu's residents generally pre-ferred the government clinic in section 26, which was maintained by the Minis-try of Health, had previously been renovated, and was soon to be supported by the reopening of the section 25 clinic.[17]

Household economics in Mpatamatu re-centred around the family member with the most stable income, irrespective of whether it was the husband or wife. This reorientation happened in light of structural changes that reduced the mine from its status as the provider of a living environment. These changes involved both a corporate retreat from the residential areas of the mine's labour force and the separation of the township's residents from its abandoned corporate social welfare buildings. Interestingly, many of the programmes that were once started to attribute to women a particular dependent socio-economic position provided those very women with the skills and knowledge they needed to help them re-place their husbands' lost income.

Practices of dependence therefore equipped these women with the skills that allowed them to cope with the collapse of the corporate structure they and their families had previously depended on. Dependence was turned upside down within families living in Mpatamatu and within the relationship between the township and its residents. As the next chapter will show, the abandoned material environment became dependent on the initiative of a particular social group, one that had previously been in a subaltern position in Mpatamatu, namely govern-ment teachers.

Notes

1. Resident of Mpatamatu, interview with the author, 11 August 2016, Mpatamatu.
2. See Prain (1956), Robinson (1967: 173–77), Mitchell (1951).
3. See Moore (1948: 125), Onselen (1976: 238), Luchembe (1982: 247–48), Meebelo (1986: 7).
4. For a detailed construction plan, see RST Roan Antelope Division (1964e: drawing 502-2348/2).
5. On the critique of the RLI, see also Kapferer (2006: 150–51).
6. See *Horizon* (1970b). Former mine clinic nurse, interview with the author, 9 July 2016, Kamfinsa; Fenia Muyutu, interview with the author, 30 August 2016, Mpatamatu; Resi-dent of Mpatamatu, interview with the author, 20 September 2016, Luanshya.
7. Fenia Muyutu, interview with the author, 30 August 2016, Mpatamatu.
8. Fenia Muyutu, community centre tour with the author, 14 September 2016, Mpatamatu.

9. Fenia Muyutu remembered the details of her job precisely, and I found them confirmed in archival material. Community development reports from 1970 and 1975 noted that '23 women [had] been enrolled for Home Maker's Course' and that 'a new course [had] started with 23 women . . .'. See RMMTMB (1970, 1975).

10. The centre was first mentioned in an RCM (1977) report on youth development in the township commissioned by RCM's personnel director. It did not appear in the earlier reports of 1970, 1974 and 1975. See RMMTMB (1970; 1974a: 3–5; 1975: 3–4).

11. The main building's structure can be traced back to the 1961 drawings attached to the 1964 appropriation request for Kabulangeti Community Centre. See RST Roan Antelope Division (1963c).

12. Devisch (1996: 573) first defined 'villagisation' in his work on Kinshasa, DRC, in the 1970s as 'a process of psychic and social endogenisation of modern city life, thus allowing the migrant to surmount the schizophrenic split between the traditional, rural and "pagan" life as against the new urban, Christian world'.

13. ZCCM's pay scale comprised six grades: G6/7 for general workers like shovelers, G5 for specialized workers like samplers, G4 for craftsmen like pumpmen, G3 for supervisors and section bosses, G2 for shift bosses and G1 for senior shift bosses. A 'U' was added to the pay grade, as in the case of Figure 2.4, for miners working underground. Boniface Mwanza, first township tour with the author, 28 April 2016, Mpatamatu.

14. Mealie meal is coarse maize flour that is made into a porridge known as *nshima* or *ubwali* by adding hot water. It is the staple food of Zambia and other parts of southern Africa.

15. Samuel Yumba, first interview with the author, 27 May 2016, Mpatamatu; second interview with the author, 6 August 2016, Mpatamatu.

16. Laurence Banda, interview with the author, 21 September 2016, Mpatamatu.

17. See United Nations Children's Emergency Fund Eastern and Southern Africa (2016). During a post-fieldwork revisit to Mpatamatu in July 2018, I found that the section 25 clinic was indeed back in service.

Chapter 3

Of Miners and Teachers

'Life was very good for the miners', said Likando Muyunda.[1] 'They lived a luxury life and were provided with everything', he continued. We were sitting on a bench outside the Ndeke congregation of the United Church of Zambia (UCZ) in the eastern part of Luanshya. The Sunday service was still under way. Prayers and songs escaped through the open doors of the church into the freshness of a Copperbelt July. Likando Muyunda had been a teacher at Mpatamatu Secondary School for more than two decades. He had been posted to the school in 1983, where he rose to head of department and ultimately held the office of head teacher from 2006 until his retirement in 2010. When I visited the school, I found his name written on the wall in a list of head teachers going back to when Zambians had been excluded from holding that office. Mpatamatu Secondary School opened as the township's first 'senior school' for Africans in 1966. Its first headmaster came from South Africa, recalled Likando Muyunda. He remembered the late 1980s as a time of great hardship in the educational sector. Salaries were low, the school was in constant need of qualified staff, and many teachers went to neighbouring countries in the south to work, some returning with a car after a term's teaching. Likando Muyunda stayed to teach and protest. He remembered taking part in large-scale strikes against price rises and social security cuts in 1987 (LeBas 2007: 240–41). However, his greatest contribution to improving the situation of teachers at the time, he explained, was when he helped to open Mpatamatu's first government clinic, initiated in the head teacher's office in Mpatamatu Secondary School in 1988. Despite the fact that government schools were integrated into corporate mine townships, medical facilities for government employees were initially absent. Teachers were referred to the shafts' first-aid stations, where, according to Likando Muyunda, they were treated as second-class patients. Access to mine facilities for teachers was revoked when Zambia Consolidated Copper Mines (ZCCM) had to cut its social spending. Eventually the makeshift clinic at Mpatamatu Secondary School was relocated to a mine house rented from ZCCM's Luanshya Division in 1989. It merged into the section 26 clinic when the mine clinic was taken over by the Ministry of Health in 2008.[2]

Likando Muyunda's memories of working in Mpatamatu offered me a different perspective on mine township life. The paternalistic practices of ZCCM did not extend to teachers. As education was important for the reproduction of the mine's labour force, schools were integrated into a corporate environment that had been developed and built for mineworkers and their dependants. However, the teachers working at the schools shared only selected aspects of the material living environment. They lived on a different socio-economic level than the parents of their pupils. Access to provisions such as health and sports facilities was not an inherent part of their employment contract. Rather, these amenities were conceded to them as outsiders who had come to live within a company town run by the mine.

How were schools and teachers integrated into the corporate mine township of Mpatamatu? What role did the township's social welfare buildings play in the changing relationship between mineworkers and teachers before and after ZCCM's privatization? This chapter follows up on my analysis of the relationship between men and women in Chapter 2. In it I revisit the pay line buildings and community centres. All these buildings had previously been material locations that set the scene for the reproduction of particular socio-economic positions among Mpatamatu's population. This corporate setting, which was based on the mine's involvement in people's lives, collapsed when ZCCM's successors in Luanshya retreated from the residential areas of their labour force.

Mpatamatu had been built as a mine township, a company town that served the mine's workforce. Mineworkers' relatively high wages, coupled with the infrastructures available to them, privileged them over other sectors of Zambia's employed population. I discuss these disparities by looking at the material living environment from the perspective of the teachers. Apart from an adult school previously run by the mine, schools in Mpatamatu have always been administered by the Ministry of Education. The selective access to the township's infrastructures, such as the social welfare buildings, shows that teachers were integrated into the mine township as second-class residents. In this sense, as a mine township Mpatamatu was not only an 'inherently exclusionary place' (Larmer and Laterza 2017: 702) when viewed from the outside, it was also exclusionary when seen from the inside, as it represented a different material environment for the teachers who lived and worked there. This arrangement changed with the breaking up of ZCCM, which marked a turning point in the relationship between mineworkers and teachers, as mineworkers and their dependants lost access to a corporate living environment. Eventually the former social welfare buildings were taken over by the teachers, who became the driving force behind projects of renovation, which included former corporate as well as government buildings.

In this chapter, I investigate the changes in the relationship between mineworkers and teachers against the backdrop of Mpatamatu as a living environment for different socio-economic groups. I follow processes of material and social ruination, that is, the corporate abandonment of welfare buildings and the socio-economic decline of mineworkers and their families as privileged residents of the township. I juxtapose these processes with the rise of teachers as renovators of buildings left behind by the mine or neglected by the Ministry of Education. The reappropriation of the mine's social welfare buildings led to a reversal of living conditions for mineworkers and teachers. While the mineworkers and their families struggled with retrenchment and the collapse of the mine's non-monetary remunerative practices, the teachers improved their socio-economic position by using abandoned corporate spaces for private educational projects. What I draw attention to here is the way in which this transition happened, a reappropriation that I see rooted in the material characteristics of the buildings and the creative ways in which the teachers modified them. Their practices mark the conversion of processes of ruination into communal material and social renovation.

Privileging Miners

The privileging of mineworkers by providing them with a material living environment based on their employment goes back to the early days of the Copperbelt as a mining area. Both a large labour force and the infrastructures to accommodate it were needed. The scale of the industrial operations involved made it feasible for mining companies to develop entire townships with social provisions. In order to safeguard the reproduction of labour, the mine extended its paternalistic care from the mine shaft and health care to its workers' houses and the social welfare buildings provided for them. I have shown in the previous chapter how much these welfare measures were based on a male order that mostly rendered women the dependants of their mineworker husbands. However, I have also illustrated how women who were employed by the mine or were engaged in economic programmes sometimes managed to cut across the gendered division of labour that prevailed at the mine.

Housing and housing allowances have been part of all formal employment in Zambia. As such, teachers accommodated in school compounds lived in an employer-provided environment comparable to that enjoyed by the mineworkers. However, the level of mineworkers' wages set them apart from all the other segments of the labour force. Monetary grants and allocations in kind increased the differences in remuneration. In fact, the extensive infrastructures within the mine townships provided the material basis for an urban life based on work, consumption and recreation. Mine employment resulted not only in a place to work and sleep, but also in new locations in which to live and socialize, from the roads leading to one's plot and the electricity and water lines connecting one's mine house via the number of rooms within it to the social welfare buildings available for after-work activities in one's township section.

When teachers were posted to Mpatamatu, they were allocated a house in the respective teachers' compound. Placed next to the schools, these compounds were separate from the mineworkers' houses. In this sense, teachers were integrated through spatial separation. Moreover, not all schools possessed such a residential quarter for their staff, usually being too small for the number of teachers they had. Many had to commute to Mpatamatu from outside. In either case, the exclusivity of the corporate mine township became an everyday experience for them. Looking at these past conditions in light of what the teachers shared with me, I feel compelled to re-engage with a Marxist marker of class that has been applied to privileged islets within a country's labour force, that is, minorities whose social reality diverged greatly from that of other workers.

Next Door to Zambia's 'Labour Aristocracy'

During his fieldwork on the Copperbelt in 1968–1972, Burawoy (1972a: 6; 2001: 533) came to see Zambia's mineworkers as a 'labour aristocracy'. He identified mineworkers as 'an elite stratum of the working class' based on their material remuneration and the corporate provisions from which they benefited (Burawoy 1972b: 277). His analysis was informed by Marxist theory in the historical context of worker unionization in England at the turn of the twentieth century.[3] The concept helped Burawoy to recognize what seemed to be a global phenomenon.

In the present case, this means a relatively prosperous part of the labour force was concerned with its own economic interests, rather than the broader political goal of decolonization. Accordingly, Zambian mineworkers were politically conservative, out of fear of losing their economic position. According to Burawoy, this became evident in two developments on the eve of national independence in 1964. First, there were no African National Congress (ANC) branches in the Copperbelt's mine townships. Secondly, mineworkers resisted the local spread and organization of the United National Independence Party (UNIP). Marxist reasoning attributed to mineworkers a lack of revolutionary consciousness (Burawoy 1972b: 277–78).

However, this analytical perspective has come under scrutiny. In his work on Zambian mineworkers, Larmer (2007: 11–15) came to the conclusion that the 'Labour Aristocracy Debate' of the early 1970s involved a structural bias. As Parpart (1983: 4–6) had noted earlier, economic, political and ideological factors had to be considered at the same time. A fixation on the structural position of mineworkers among the wage-earning population left no room to grasp conceptually divergent practices, solidarity with non-mineworkers or wage redistributions from industrial to rural areas.

Nonetheless, 'labour aristocracy' continued to be used widely to classify the particular socio-economic and socio-political status of Zambia's mineworkers before ZCCM's privatization in 1997.[4] In my view, these more recent uses of the term 'labour aristocracy' were less concerned with mineworkers' political positions than with describing a class that had access to corporate welfare measures and that passed its jobs on within the family like an inheritance. It is this understanding of 'labour aristocracy' that others, like Parry (1999: 112), have applied to similarly privileged parts of local workforces in other parts of the world.

I would like to tilt the concept of 'labour aristocracy' further away from suggestions concerning mineworkers' political leanings towards a relative assessment of their material living conditions vis-à-vis other members of the workforce. With regard to her own upbringing, Mususa (2014: 6) reported that families with access to the mines' welfare system 'were the most protected'. In light of my fieldwork, I suggest redeploying 'labour aristocracy' in order to carve out the material and economic differences in the life-worlds of Mpatamatu's residents, whether they were employed by the mine or by the Ministry of Education. I do so by juxtaposing mineworkers' and teachers' access to the township's social welfare buildings before and after ZCCM's privatization. Obviously, the concept is temporally limited to the time before 1997, a period when the mine maintained its presence in the township and provided economic subsidies and social amenities, a time when the lowest wage in the mining industry was above the highest wage in any other industrial sector (Burawoy 1972b: 278).[5]

Mpatamatu Secondary School's former head teacher, Likando Muyunda, pointed to several inequalities between mineworkers and teachers during his time of service. Mail was delivered to mine houses, whereas teachers had to collect their letters from the office of the District Education Board Secretary in Luanshya. In comparison to his salary in the 1980s, he referred to mineworkers' as enjoying 'double payment'. They were in a position to purchase commodities at the level of a teacher's monthly income. He remembered that they would occasionally leave their payslips in the teachers' compounds to emphasize their higher socio-economic status.

Mineworkers' wages were a reference point, but an unattainable one. When their wages were increased, it was a trigger for subsequent labour action across other sectors (Bates 1971: 68). The teachers' impression that they were being mistreated was exacerbated by the fact that the majority of mineworkers acquired only a low level of formal education. Moreover, they were entitled to live in company towns, something unimaginable for teachers, who had to go through postings to a rural area. Mine jobs often remained within a mineworker's family. Teachers had to face these contrasts, Likando Muyunda explained, when they were posted to a government school in a mine township.

Positioning Teachers

Mine townships like Mpatamatu were highly homogeneous residential areas. Based on the 1966 *Brown Report*, Bates (1971: 111–12) calculated that only 5 per cent of residents of the Nkana mine township in Kitwe were not employed by the mine. Similar conditions existed in Luanshya's mine townships of Roan and Mpatamatu. No residential houses, apart from the teachers' compounds, were constructed for those not employed by the mine. Collings and Schaerer originally planned to have at least one school for each of Mpatamatu's sections (RACM 1957: appendix, map NR.RA1). Teachers were nonetheless in an absolute minority.

Zambia's first Minister of Education, John Mwanakatwe (1968: 51), noted that the mining companies 'played the most important role in the building programme' for primary schools. Ultimately schools were only constructed in the sections of Mpatamatu developed before the nationalization of Zambia's copper industry in 1969/1970. As such, the distribution of schools in Mpatamatu followed the general pattern of the township's spatial organization and elaborateness, as well as its provision with social facilities noted earlier in Chapter 1.

Like mineworkers, teachers entered the township by virtue of their occupation. The teachers' compounds were located next to the schools, just as the township was placed next to the shafts. The structural situation was complex. Teachers lived in houses built by the mine, located in a company town and administered by the government. Mpatamatu's first school was constructed together with the mine houses in section 21 in 1957. Mpatamatu Primary School was opened as a 'government school for natives' in 1959.[6] At the same time, Roan Antelope Copper Mines (RACM) provided adult education in its own mine school in section 23; see Figure 1.2, centre). Newly enrolled workers were taught to read and write before they entered the mine's services.[7] In the first half of the 1960s, four schools followed in sections 22 and 24, Mwaiseni, Nkulumashiba, Kansumbi and Nkambo Primary Schools. In the late 1960s, before the Baluba extension of the township, Mpatamatu possessed five government primary schools, one for each of the existing sections 21 to 25 (see Map 0.1).

Collings and Schaerer included one 'senior school' in their plans for the township. Mpatamatu Secondary School was opened at the township's central roundabout in 1966, changing the educational prospects for Mpatamatu's population. Reforms in the 1970s introduced 'basic education' as the new minimum standard for government schools (Alexander 1983: 209, appendix 2, 21). It was not until decades later that schools with seven grades were expanded to include the eighth and ninth grades. In 1983 the Ministry of Education took over the mine school in section 23, converting it into Nkulumashiba Secondary School.[8] In 2011 the Patriotic Front (PF) government under Michael Sata reversed the decision on basic education, going back to seven years of primary and five years of secondary school education. As many pupils did not pass the examination after grade 7 to move on to secondary school, Mpatamatu's primary schools continued to run classes up to grade 9. In fact, they remained basic schools. In 2012, Nkulumashiba Primary School, which had previously also been upgraded to a basic school, started to phase out its lower grades and became Mpatamatu's third senior school, Nkulumashiba East Secondary School.[9] What became evident from these developments in the educational sector was that the presence of the Ministry of Education in Mpatamatu increased. However, the working and living conditions of teachers did not improve as a result.

Township development and the construction of schools were interrelated processes. An initial number of schools had been intended in the spatial layout for Mpatamatu. They were not isolated or on the periphery of the township but were built in the middle of the sections in proximity to the mineworkers' houses. This resulted in the existence of two distinct socio-economic life-worlds side by side. In his article on the 1970 teachers' strike, Kanduza noted that living next door to the labour aristocracy was 'disturbing' for teachers. Their accommodation was inferior and turned into material markers magnified by the differences in wages and amenities tied to employment:

> Even in the Copperbelt where the miners were the best-housed workers in the country, accommodation for teachers was of comparatively inferior quality. This was particularly disturbing since the teachers compared themselves to the miners who had electrified houses for very small monthly charges and a free water supply. (Kanduza 1981: 497–98)

I witnessed these differences in quality during my own fieldwork in Mpatamatu. When I visited research participants at home, I tried to discuss housing issues with them. In a conversation on the different types of mine houses with the miner-teacher couple introduced earlier in Chapter 2, the husband drew detailed plans of the houses he was allocated during his service for the mine. His drawings were so accurate that I would later match them with the original building plans for three different house types I found at the archives. We compared the mine houses to the teacher's compound house he lived in with his wife, who was a primary school teacher in Mpatamatu. The construction materials used for the houses were mainly the same: brick walls and asbestos roofing. However, there were spatial differences and one central function that set teachers' houses apart from most mineworker accommodation. Mine houses generally had an in-house toilet and shower. This was not the case for the houses in that particular teachers' compound: both were located in a shelter separate from the house.

Teachers explained to me that under ZCCM the differences in material living conditions were reduced by admitting teachers to the township's social welfare buildings. Clubs, taverns and sports facilities were now open to them, though understandably full membership of a mine club was not available. Having a drink with colleagues or friends at a beer hall and playing volleyball at the sports complex was apparently quite common. The mine's social provisions in Mpatamatu were relatively open at that time. Initially, this included the mine's health facilities.

In light of Likando Muyunda's account of the establishment of Mpatamatu's first government clinic, I came to understand that this openness decreased towards the terminal years of Zambia's Second Republic (1972–1991) and ZCCM (1982–1997). The financial situation of the parastatal was now chained to the national budget, as the World Bank's structural adjustment programme required greater austerity on the part of the government. This influenced ZCCM's budget: social spending was cut, a development that intensified with the prospective reprivatization of the copper sector prepared in the first years of the Third Republic.[10]

Teachers' experiences in Mpatamatu showed me that their material living environment was changing in relation to their access to the mine's social welfare buildings. The integration of teachers into the township depended on the general economic outlook and corporate policy. It increased when copper mining became a national endeavour after the government took over the industry. Corporate paternalism was extended to residents of Mpatamatu who did not work for the mine. However, this inclusiveness was revoked when financial constraints made it hard to maintain even existing amenities for mineworkers and their dependants. The integration of teachers into Mpatamatu decreased. However, the exclusion of teachers and the renewed orientation towards the mine's labour force did not save the mine townships and their social provisions.

Replacing Miners

Mpatamatu gradually lost its corporate character after the privatization of ZCCM's Luanshya Division. The downscaling of mining operations and the retrenchment of mineworkers transformed Mpatamatu from a mine township that had followed developments underground to a satellite town distant from Luanshya town centre. The municipality took over the township's administration. Mine houses were sold to retrenched mineworkers as part of their terminal benefits. The township and its infrastructures ceased to be an extension of the mine from the site of extraction to the site of the workforce's social existence and living environment. Mpatamatu's social welfare buildings fell idle.

Buildings abandoned or deemed expendable by the mine attracted the attention of the teachers. In contrast to the majority of mineworkers, they remained in employment. Their salaries even improved under the Movement for Multi-Party Democracy (MMD) government of Frederick Chiluba (1943–2011) from 1991 to 2002. In comparison to those who continued to work in the mining sector as contract labour, teachers could rely on relatively stable employment by the Ministry of Education. This made room for economic activities outside their immediate family household. Laid off and often left to wait for the disbursement of their terminal benefits, many mineworkers went into subsistence farming. Those who managed to remain in formal mine employment struggled to break even in the face of the privatization of former mine infrastructures such as water, electricity and sewerage. Mineworkers had to pay bills previously unknown to them. In contrast to teachers, moreover, they were not in any position to start a business.

Teachers were attracted by the social welfare buildings' spatial characteristics. In the years following ZCCM's privatization, these particular parts of the corporate welfare infrastructure were reappropriated by this particular group of government employees. The community centres possessed a classroom structure, while the pay line buildings had the potential to be split into separate rooms. Moreover, teachers were motivated by the need for additional educational facilities in Mpatamatu. Buildings that had marked the privileged status of the mine's labour force and that had complemented their financial remuneration materially were transformed into private educational projects driven by the teachers, a previously disadvantaged part of the township's population. In a process of resetting the socio-economic positions of different social groups in Mpatamatu, teachers replaced mineworkers in respect of their privileged relationship with the material environment of the township. Among the locations that had been symbols of the labour aristocracy were Mpatamatu's pay line buildings on the main road leading into the township, two identical, long flat halls that had been built in the early 1960s and 1970s.[11]

Samuel Yumba, a former mineworker who received his monthly salary at the buildings between 1985 and the late 1990s, when RAMCOZ introduced bank transactions, provided me with a perspective on the buildings' past when we visited the former pay line together. On the first day of every month, mine and federal police secured the buildings and prepared them for the wage payments. Poles along the fence in front of the main gate forced the mineworkers into a queue. The gate formed a physical bottleneck allowing policemen to check the inflow and outflow of people one by one. Holding German shepherd dogs on leashes, the policemen were an intimidating presence. They requested mine ID cards and sent in mineworkers in groups of ten to twenty. The mineworkers walked along the buildings' outer walls, lining up on the western side of each pay line building. Mine ID numbers written above the doors indicated when it was their turn to proceed into the halls. Inside, they received their monthly payslip and a voucher, before finally being given their salaries in cash.[12]

At the time of my fieldwork, groups of pupils usually stood in the bright sunlight in front of the doors leading into the buildings. They peeked through the broken and bent wire netting of the fence surrounding the pay line buildings, a relic of the former high-security environment. On Sundays, prayers and songs coming out of the buildings were audible from afar. The long halls had been divided into separate classrooms with plywood: nine rooms, one for each of Suzika Private School's grades 1 to 9 (see Figure 3.1). The school had been founded by Fackson Mugala, a former head teacher at Kansumbi Primary School, at Kabulangeti Community Centre in 1997. It was extended and eventually relocated to the pay line buildings in 2001.[13]

The plywood walls were covered with pupils' graffiti. Holes had been drilled into them, allowing schoolmates on the other side to be seen. Simple steel and wooden benches filled the rooms, orientated towards blackboards screwed to the dry walls. After spending some time in the buildings, it became obvious to me that they had not been designed for students to sit and study for several hours a day. Little light entered through the gap between the outer walls and the roof truss, and the compartmentalized space quickly became sticky. The roof radiated considerable heat during the dry season, turning the inside into an oven.

The pay line buildings were really made for miners, entering when it was their turn, collecting what they had to collect, and going out again after a short period of time. After the corporate abandonment of Mpatamatu, the buildings' roofed spaces represented something valuable for the township's community, and the ability to divide these spaces into classrooms overruled any other material or spatial disadvantages for the new tenants. Likewise, the former community centres invited the teachers to reappropriate them, their spatial order and material durability promoting the foundation of new educational institutions. The centres

Figure 3.1. Classroom of Suzika Private School in section 21's former pay line buildings. Photo by the author.

offered separate rooms under one roof and spacious plots surrounding them. In the following paragraphs, I revisit Mpatamatu's three community centres and describe how they were reappropriated by teachers after ceasing to be the workplace for women like Fenia Muyutu (see Chapter 2).

Happyson Kaunda took over Kansengu Community Centre in 1997. At the time, he was a teacher at Mpatamatu Secondary School. He rented the main building and the adjacent library from RAMCOZ (see Figure 3.2). His plan was to found an integrated pre-, primary and secondary school recalling the main building's prior function as a pre-school.[14] However, Happyson Kaunda's ideas for Kansengu Community Centre encountered resistance. The mine's first operator after ZCCM's privatization, RAMCOZ, had amassed huge debts. Its financial difficulties, eventual bankruptcy and liquidation resulted in the separation of the mine from its social assets.

The receiver of RAMCOZ's social assets planned to sell them off in order to cover the outstanding financial claims. The former social welfare buildings represented commercial assets, and solvent buyers were preferred over sitting tenants using and maintaining the buildings with whatever means at hand. The case of Kansengu Community Centre illustrates how the formerly corporate social welfare infrastructure was dismantled like the parastatal ZCCM. The library (see Figure 3.2, right building) was given to the Zambia Electricity Supply Corporation (ZESCO) to house its local branch office in the western half of the building, where residents could buy units for their electricity meters at home. The eastern part of the building was sublet to the Luanshya Municipal Council (LMC), to serve as an office for collecting land rates, a real-estate tax based on the value of the plot and the house on it, which had to be paid by all house-owners in Mpatamatu.[15]

Martin Kasonso and his father bought the main building of the Kansengu Community Centre from the receiver (see Figure 3.2, left building). Father and son both worked in education: the father had been a teacher at Mpatamatu Secondary School, while Martin Kasonso was the training manager and deputy director at the Northern Technical College (NORTEC) in Ndola. In conversation with me, they admitted that they had different ideas about how to use the for-

Figure 3.2. Former Kansengu Community Centre in section 21. Photo by the author.

mer centre's main building. Their plans ranged from using it in its past function as a community centre on a non-profit basis to founding a commercial private college. These ideas had been informed by the building's past position in the township. Martin Kasonso's desire to re-establish the centre as a welfare facility in the service of Mpatamatu's residents has to be seen in light of his biography and upbringing in the township.

Martin Kasonso was born in 1973. His mother was a nurse at Luanshya's mine clinics, and his father was a government teacher. His mother's job allowed the family to access the township's corporate infrastructures. With both his parents working, Martin Kasonso was sent to pre-school at Kabulangeti and Kansengu Community Centres from 1977 to 1978. In 1979 he entered Nkulumashiba Primary School. He conveyed a very positive image of those pre- and primary school years and the opportunities he had as a young child growing up in the mine township. He regularly went to the library, played table tennis, and became interested in boxing. These activities were no longer available to children growing up in Mpatamatu at the time of my fieldwork. Eventually, he passed his grade 7 exams and left the township for secondary education in 1986.[16]

Martin Kasonso re-engaged with his former community through the sale of Kansengu Community Centre. He invested considerably in renovating the centre's main building. At the time of my fieldwork, it mostly stood empty, though it was tended by a caretaker. From time to time, ward development council meetings, a local-level municipal organ, took place there. The building cast a positive projection into the future by reproducing ideas of its past use and defying the surrounding processes of material ruination.

In 1997 Fackson Mugala founded Suzika Private School in the Kabulangeti Community Centre in section 24. A primary school teacher from Northern Province, he was first posted to Luanshya in 1981. In 1984 he was transferred to Kansumbi Primary School in Mpatamatu for the first time. Over the years, he climbed the hierarchy and returned to Kansumbi Primary School as head teacher in 2007, an office he held until 2011.[17]

Fackson Mugala started his private school at a time when the former social welfare buildings had been abandoned by the mine and the government schools had a bad reputation. Underfunded and understaffed government schools could not prepare children sufficiently to pass exams on the way to secondary education. Fackson Mugala started tutoring pupils for grade 7 examinations. Eventually he founded a separate school in the rooms of the former community centre. The school's programme gradually expanded to include pre-, primary and secondary school classes.

Founding a school at a former social welfare building was not without its risks. Fackson Mugala was the sitting tenant of the Kabulangeti Community Centre, not its owner. In receivership, RAMCOZ constantly put all its social assets up for sale. In 2014 he received a letter of offer for the centre and invited

three friends to pool money in order to raise the capital. What started as a financial project resulted in the foundation of the Mpatamatu College of Education
(MPACE) (see Figure 3.3). The four investors made the initial payment and were
still paying monthly instalments at the time of my fieldwork. The centre was
renovated and became the campus of their new college. This case illustrates the
change in the financial position of teachers vis-à-vis miners in Mpatamatu.

According to Fackson Mugala, students were instructed in three classrooms,
together with a science lab and a computer lab, rooms that had once been used to
teach women how to become 'modern' housewives. The former pre-school shelters were turned into another classroom and library. A separate toilet annex was
built to replace the broken sanitary block in the building. MPACE's vegetable
garden at the back of the main building was run by the students. The teaching
of skills in subsistence farming was both a reference to the former women's clubs
and to the increasing dominance of agriculture in people's lives in Mpatamatu.
Apart from the numerous farming plots that spread over the township's previously undeveloped or discarded land, this provided another example of 'the bush'
coming to the town and of the continuity of agricultural subsistence in this os-
tensibly planned urban environment.

Happyson Kaunda started a second school project at former Muliashi Community Centre in section 26. Joyce Muleya, head teacher of Golden Eagle Private
School since 2003, could still recall the building's former uses, as she had participated in a tailoring class there in 1994.[18] The school's presence in the centre was
related to its previous educational purpose and to the infrastructural differences
between the west and east of Mpatamatu. While the mine had equipped sections
21 to 25 with five primary and one secondary school, there had been no government schools north of Nkulumashiba Stream in sections 26 and 27.

Collings and Schaerer's original township plan had been based on the principle that facilities should be in close proximity to mine houses. Although Mpata-

Figure 3.3. Mpatamatu College of Education at former Kabulangeti Community Centre.
Photo by the author.

matu was close to the shafts, the social welfare buildings were supposed to be constructed near their users' accommodation.[19] Long before the Ministry of Education came in and built a school in section 27, Golden Eagle Private School was chosen by many of my research participants living in sections 26 and 27 for their children to start schooling. The absence of a government school marked a departure in the township development process from the original conception of each township section as a 'small socially self-contained residential unit' (RACM 1957: 6). Land had been reserved for a school in section 27. However, three decades passed before Kalulu Primary School was eventually opened in 2011.[20]

Joyce Muleya managed pre-school and primary school classes from grades 1 to 7. Golden Eagle Private School was an examination centre for pupils wanting to move on to grade 8 at secondary level. Joyce Muleya explained that the school had around a hundred pupils in total, spread over one class in each of the seven grades. School fees were set at 180 Kwacha per three-month term, a sum fewer than a quarter of parents could come up with. A shortage of funds was therefore a problem here, as in the township's government schools. She made it clear that sometimes teachers went home with only a month's salary for a whole term.

One of the school's teachers explained to me how the school mapped current needs onto the past use of the building's rooms.[21] We were sitting in the head teacher's office, the former workplace of the 'CD' (community development) officer. Where young people had played table tennis, pupils of grades 1, 3 and 7 were learning their lessons. The storeroom was still located in the middle section, right next to what had been the offices of the head teacher and the pre-school teachers. Grades 2, 4 and 6 and the pre-school were housed in the eastern wing. The separate classroom buildings that used to house the community centre's pre-school were being used as a grade 5 classroom and a storeroom. The teacher's account showed how the material world of corporate paternalism dissolved into a post-reprivatization world of private initiatives.

Muliashi Community Centre was occasionally used for vaccination campaigns by section 26 clinic staff and for meetings of the ward development council. In preparation for the 2016 presidential elections, the football pitch next to the centre served as a meeting place for local party groups.[22] Present and past appropriations of township spaces interacted with each other again and again. Open fields in the mine townships had been used for political meetings since the 1935 Copperbelt strike (Russell 1935: 22–23, 25, 29).

On 11 August 2016, I witnessed township residents walking up to the former community centre and casting their votes in the presidential election. It was astonishing to observe this most fundamental practice of participatory democracy being made possible by the existence of corporate remains. Moreover, other former social welfare buildings, such as the sports complex and the section 25 mine clinic, were also being used as polling stations.[23] Spaces to meet and pursue collective action were in high demand in Mpatamatu.

In the case of the former pay line buildings and community centres, teachers succeeded the mining company as managers of the former social welfare buildings, replacing the mineworkers and their dependants as users of these facilities. The integration of work, accommodation and social welfare in Mpatamatu was atomized. Many mineworkers were left only with their privatized mine houses. Teachers' projects, by contrast, reintegrated isolated buildings into the township community, making them usable and accessible again for Mpatamatu's residents.

Mineworkers were replaced at the former social welfare buildings and turned into farmers, with some even becoming teachers themselves. I met one of these miners-turned-teachers at one of Mpatamatu's primary schools. He was born into a mineworker's family in 1969. His father had worked for the Roan Selection Trust (RST), Roan Consolidated Mines (RCM) and ZCCM for three decades. He received his primary education at the Luanshya Trust School from 1975 to 1981, a corporate school previously reserved for the children of expatriate mineworkers.[24] In 1990 he followed his father and joined ZCCM to work as a planning clerk. As the situation worsened under RAMCOZ, he realized that he needed to change his occupation. 'The mine did everything in the past, but at the time the mine was unable [to do so]', he recalled. A child evangelist at UCZ, he thought of becoming a teacher. After receiving his terminal benefits in 2002, he attended a teacher training college for two years. His first posting took him to Luapula Province. In 2011 he returned to Mpatamatu where he has been teaching ever since.[25] In the most literal sense, a teacher had replaced a mineworker on an individual level.

Renovating Teachers

Teachers revived Mpatamatu's former social welfare buildings by reappropriating, maintaining and renovating them. At the same time, they kept the township's government schools alive. They struggled to prevent the ransacking of the township's infrastructures, particularly government property. Mpatamatu's schools were old, most having been in continuous use without major maintenance work since being opened. The schools' brick walls had seen more than five decades of mineworkers' children going in and out.

In a rare case, Mpatamatu Secondary School received additional classroom blocks through a World Bank programme in the 1970s. At the time of my fieldwork, these buildings too needed renovation, as Chishimba Kambwili (2008), Member of Parliament for the Roan constituency, pointed out in the National Assembly. Other schools like Mwaiseni Primary School had been freshly painted, a superficial measure that was possible because the school building's material substance had generally withstood the elements. The real challenges were the small classrooms, the dysfunctional sanitary facilities and the intermittent water and electricity supply.

Traces of ransacking dated back to the early 2000s. Mineworker families struggled with the social ruination following the retrenchments. People started raiding mine and government property in search of building materials that they could use themselves or resell to traders. Shattered school windows often remained broken, because the glass had been stolen. Bricks, window frames, metal furniture and pipes were also purloined. When a teacher at Kansumbi Primary School took me on a school tour, I became aware of how far the ransacking had gone. People had cut down the school's flagpole and stolen it. This was dystopian: the flagpole was not just an iron rod with a piece of textile blowing at its top – it held the national flag of Zambia, the focus of every school assembly, centre of an institution that was supposed to educate future generations.[26]

What international investors pursued on a corporate scale, people repeated more privately. It occurred to me that the asset-stripping of Luanshya's mine for scrap metal by Binani Industries' subsidiary RAMCOZ had spread to Mpatamatu. The mine township as a company town became a ruin of corporate paternalism, though still a ruin in which people tried to make a living. This echoed Dawdy's (2010: 777) conclusion that ruins do not represent a *terra nullius*. As in the case of Edensor's (2005b: 23–24) field sites, corporate material remains in Mpatamatu became 'resource areas that [provided] architectural plunder for scavengers and collectors'. People continued to live in the material environment that surrounded them. However, what had once been built and maintained for the labour force was taken apart in its abandonment and dysfunction. Mpatamatu's social welfare buildings marked the boundary between devouring the past in the face of economic hardship and preserving the past through alternative reappropriations for a better future.

The fact that people turned to schools to make a living shocked me, giving me a glimpse into the conditions of life in Mpatamatu in the early 2000s. The situation was grave, asserted the teacher who stared at the remnants of the flagpole with me. She remembered how her family had shared mealie meal with neighbouring mineworker families. Some of her students still missed classes because they had to contribute to their family's income. The exclusive space to which Likando Muyunda had introduced me at the beginning of this chapter had disappeared. Teachers had to protect their workplaces from those who had to resort to making a living as 'scavengers and collectors'.

At schools in Mpatamatu, the teachers used the meagre funds raised through parent-teacher associations to employ security guards. All schools were in the process of either erecting or refurbishing existing fences around their compounds. In the face of the socio-economic decline of mineworkers' families and the material ruination of Mpatamatu, the imaginary walls surrounding the former home of the labour aristocracy had closed in on those locations that still had a regular source of income amidst a discarded part of Zambia's industrial workforce.

Stoler's concept of 'ruination' directs attention to the aftermath and durabilities of imperial formations. From the perspective of Mpatamatu, the concept
encompasses the material remnants of corporate paternalism, such as a former
community centre; the 'act' of ruination, that is, the disintegration of the township as a company town; the 'condition' of being ruined, that is, the living conditions and the state of infrastructures; and the 'cause' of the decay of the material
living environment in the township, that is, the reprivatization of the mine without continuing its social investment or handing it over properly to private service
providers or the state (Stoler 2016: 350). In light of these multiple aspects of
'ruination', the concept reveals the different temporalities related to the former
social welfare buildings and grasps the force of ruinous processes, from material
decay to social decline.

However, the semantics of 'ruination' cannot account for the *creative* ways in
which teachers reappropriated the former social welfare buildings. Founding private schools goes beyond the question of what the residents of Mpatamatu were
left with. Teachers had not been left with abandoned social welfare buildings. At
a time when farming activities increased, they reappropriated unused built spaces
and removed buildings from their corporate integration. 'Ruination' as a process
was the scene of their actions. Could the concept account for their creative actions countering the very same process? Teachers' newly founded private schools
ignited an entirely different process of renovative community restructuring.

I was inspired by P. Gupta's investigation of the creative reappropriation of
leisured spaces in postcolonial Beira (Mozambique) in accounting conceptually
for teachers' reappropriations of Mpatamatu's former social welfare buildings. I
came to understand the teachers' projects in the former pay line buildings and
the community centres as 'distinct forms of renovation amidst ruination' (Gupta
2019: 135). Towns, including their abandoned buildings, represented sites of
resourcefulness.

P. Gupta rooted the concept of 'renovation' in two ways. First, building on
Stoler's (2008b: 203) usage of Lévi-Strauss's (1966: 16–21) term *bricoleur*, she
underlined the capacity of individuals to tinker with their material environment.
Second, she distinguished two separate practices within processes of 'renovation':
to *revive* a building through new ways of using it, and to *restore* previous usages in
the present. In this sense, Gupta (2019: 129–30, 133–34) followed the multiple
temporalities that were accessible through 'ruination' by looking at abandonment, decay, reappropriation and repair simultaneously.

I observed the revival and restorative aspect of 'renovation' in the reappropriation practices of the teachers. Abandoned buildings were revived, and teachers
made them useful again. Spaces were divided and new rooms established. By
founding private schools, teachers restored previous aspects of the former social welfare buildings. Education opened up a dialogue between the community

centres' past, present and future. Nostalgia for Mpatamatu's corporate past shimmered through the ways in which teachers reappropriated the centres.

Teachers re-established relationships between Mpatamatu's residents and the material remnants of their previous living environment. This is where I see a third aspect of 'renovation': to *renew*. The pay line buildings and community centres had been disconnected from the mine and its once privileged labour force. The teachers' projects of renovation brought together the materiality of the former social welfare buildings and the communal necessities of Mpatamatu's residents. This link *renewed* Mpatamatu as a municipal place in which to live by reintegrating the buildings into residents' lives.

In summary, I saw teachers in Mpatamatu involve themselves in four renovation projects. These endeavours ranged from the reappropriation of buildings to serving as a representative of their sitting tenants, and from the corporate past of Mpatamatu to the township's municipal present. Firstly, teachers supported the reappropriation of the social welfare buildings after they had been left behind by the mine. This activity involved their participation in club committees and the organization of the sitting tenants' association. They thus replaced mineworkers who had been affected by material and social ruination. Secondly, they stepped into an administrative vacuum that had been left by the mine and not closed by the municipality, reacting to township residents' needs by reusing existing buildings. Thirdly, the foundation of private schools revived the abandoned buildings and created new alternatives to the existing educational facilities in the township. This was despite the fact that these schools were just as limited by budgetary constraints as the underfunded government schools. Finally, and in my eyes most importantly, the teachers reintegrated the former social welfare buildings into the community around them. Materially they reappropriated, reopened and renovated the buildings. Temporally, they took up aspects of the buildings' prior corporate functions, interweaving past experiences, present nostalgia and future prospects. After the mine had discarded both the community and the infrastructures within it, the teachers renewed the relationship that Mpatamatu's residents once had with their material living environment.

Notes

1. Likando Muyunda, interview with the author, 31 July 2016, Luanshya.
2. Section 26 clinic staff member, interview with the author, 9 May 2016, Mpatamatu.
3. For a detailed treatise of the 'labour aristocracy theory' in the context of postcolonial Africa, see Mijere (1985: 13–32).
4. See Lee (2009: 657), Fraser (2010: 9), Macmillan (2012: 542).
5. See also Figure 4.1 'African average earnings by sector, 1954–66' in Knight (1971: 95).
6. Teacher at Mpatamatu Primary School, interview with the author, 9 August 2016, Mpatamatu.

7. Wisdom Zulu, interview with the author, 18 September 2016, Mpatamatu. On 'Adult Education in the Mining Industry', see Mwanakatwe (1968: 148–50).

8. Teacher at Nkulumashiba Secondary School, interview with the author, 13 July 2016, Mpatamatu. See also Mulenga (undated).

9. Teacher at Nkulumashiba East Secondary School, interview with the author, 12 July 2016, Mpatamatu.

10. See Simutanyi (1996), Larmer (2005: 30), Gewald and Soeters (2010: 157–58).

11. See RACM (1962: 1), RST Roan Antelope Division (1962c: 2), RCM Luanshya Division (1971).

12. Samuel Yumba, site inspection with the author, 30 May 2016, Mpatamatu.

13. Fackson Mugala, first interview with the author, 28 April 2016, Mpatamatu.

14. Happyson Kaunda, second interview with the author, 29 August 2016, Luanshya.

15. ZESCO Human Resource Officer, interview with the author, 28 September 2016, Luanshya.

16. Martin Kasonso, interview with the author, 27 September 2016, Ndola.

17. Mugala (2016); field notes by author, 8 June 2016.

18. Joyce Muleya, interview with the author, 25 July 2016, Mpatamatu.

19. The fact that children from sections 26 and 27 had to cross Nkulumashiba Stream on their way to school led to a terrible accident during the rainy season of 1995/1996. Four children drowned while crossing the river. As I discovered in the files of the Roan Mpatamatu Mine Township Management Board (RMMTMB), bridges over the river downstream from Kalulu Street bridge had apparently been an issue in the township for some time. See RMMTMB (1977).

20. Teacher at Kalulu Primary School, interview with the author, 23 September 2016, Mpatamatu.

21. Teacher at Golden Eagle Private School, interview with the author, 23 September 2016, Mpatamatu. See RST Roan Antelope Division (1963c: drawing number 518-1581/3) for a 1961 plan for a 'Women's Welfare Centre' in Mpatamatu, attached to the 1963 appropriation request to build Kabulangeti Community Centre in section 24. Muliashi and Makoma Community Centre (in Roan) were based on the same plan.

22. The ruling PF and the opposition parties, the UPND and the Rainbow Party, were active in Mpatamatu, holding rallies and running poster campaigns in the township.

23. Field notes by the author, 11 August 2016.

24. At the time of my fieldwork, Luanshya Trust School was still in corporate hands, being run by CLM. See Confucius Institute at the University of Zambia (2018).

25. Resident of Mpatamatu, interview with the author, 21 June 2016, Mpatamatu.

26. Teacher at Kansumbi Primary School, interview with the author, 8 June 2016, Mpatamatu.

Chapter 4

Of Miners and Preachers

'Miners are not used to drinking *chibuku*', asserted the man next to me.[1] 'They drank bottled beer', he added. I was sitting next to a committee member of Mpatamatu's Buseko Recreation Club on the club's premises near the main road leading into the township. Two large trees provided shade for the men drinking a few metres away from us. Our conversation was interspersed with observations about the play of light and shadow on the dusty ground in the afternoon sun, the 'shaky' economic prospects of a town like Luanshya, which was still dependent on the mine, and the group of men, many of them former mineworkers, each sipping from a plastic cup filled with *chibuku* from a shared white plastic bottle. 'We cannot blame the government, we cannot blame the Chinese investors. We can only blame the price at the London Metal Exchange', continued the committee member, reflecting on the current economic situation.[2]

It was May 2016; the copper price remained below US$5,000 per metric ton, and the Baluba underground mine was still closed. However, my interlocutor wanted me to pay attention to something else: social decline. We were sitting in a former miners' club. Buseko had been the epitome of the mineworkers' status as a labour aristocracy. Now things had changed dramatically: the men sitting in front of the decrepit club building would not buy a bottle of *chibuku* for themselves. Common situations in the past, when mineworkers drank lager from glass bottles in exclusive areas and were given amenities in kind at the club, had vanished into the white plastic bottle like a genie. The interplay of material and social ruination had many faces in Mpatamatu. At the Buseko Club, it was present in the material state of the club building, the loss of its central status under corporate paternalism and the everyday practice of consuming beer.[3]

This chapter opens with alcohol consumption as a form of after-work leisure in the African mine townships of Luanshya. I look at beer drinking from two different perspectives: as a social institution brought to urban areas by its migrant residents, and as a corporate attempt by the mine to gain control over the labour force. Beer halls and social clubs marked the beginning of a corporate infra-structure dedicated to leisure. From bars and clubs, I go on to discuss sport and its respective material sites in Mpatamatu. I continue my analysis of corporate paternalism and how it materially penetrated social life in Mpatamatu. However, at this point I also ask to what extent the structured provisions of leisure were accepted by the township population and were effective for purposes of corpo-rate social control. Prayer houses represented alternatives to the leisure facilities provided by the mine. The presence of Pentecostal churches has been growing steadily in Mpatamatu since the mine abandoned the township and its former corporate infrastructures. It is no wonder that several former social welfare build-ings, among them a tavern and the sports complex, have been turned into houses of prayer. In this sense, the preachers I write about in this chapter followed the teachers mentioned in Chapter 3 by taking over buildings that had previously been reserved for the privileged workforce of the mine. Moreover, some mine-workers have themselves become clergymen.

Miners Drinking

'Beer halls', also called 'beer parlours' and later 'taverns' or simply 'bars', con-stituted the starting point for the Copperbelt mines' infrastructure of leisure. According to Ambler and Crush (1992: 2), the corporate practice of using alco-hol and its distribution as a means of social control became established among mining companies throughout colonial southern Africa. Corporate and munici-pal authorities saw the consumption of alcohol as a source of revenue and social control, but also of social unrest. The urge to direct the drinking behaviour of Africans has to be seen in connection with corporate and government attempts to establish new 'temporal and spatial orders corresponding to the requirements of capitalist industrial development' (Ambler and Crush 1992: 21). Drinking was permitted *at* a beer hall *after* work.

The beer halls were tightly controlled locations meant to centralize an every-day practice within a delimited place of leisure in a mine township. During his fieldwork in Broken Hill (now Kabwe) in 1939/1940, Wilson documented the authorities' attempts to control beer consumption by providing alcohol only at a beer hall under European supervision.

Owing to the correlation between beer-drinking and crimes of violence in town the authorities supply a mild brew and do not trust the Africans to drink even this by themselves. They attempt to ensure that drinking is carried out in a beer hall under the eye of a European manager, with the police at the other end of the telephone. The necessity for constant European supervision makes the provision of more than one beer-hall uneconomic, since each new hall would need a separate European manager. The laws against home brewing and the possession of beer, finally, are retained in the mistaken idea that an ineffective law is better than none. (Wilson 1942: 33)

Women were integrated into Luanshya's African mine township Roan through agricultural subsistence work. Roan Antelope Copper Mines (RACM) introduced tribal elders to represent the community and solve domestic disputes (Epstein 1958: 26–47). Beer halls established another link between the mine townships and rural areas. Richards (1969: 76–77) described beer drinking among the Bemba in Northern Province as providing not only a foodstuff rich in vitamin B, but also a 'kind of entertainment' and 'the essential way of fulfilling social obligations' that was at the centre of communal festivities, an assessment also made by Moore (1948: 51) two decades earlier. Ambler and Crush (1992: 2) asserted that the availability of alcohol at the beer hall established 'a continuity of social and ritual life between the countryside and the town'. This connection between the labour force's rural origins and urban residence was considered 'essential' by RACM's first African compound manager, Spearpoint (1937: 30).

The mining company's awareness of the social meaning of beer drinking resulted in the construction of a separate beer hall in the African mine township of Roan. It emerged that beer halls were not merely drinking places, they also represented 'social centres' (Moore 1948: 51) that produced 'a distinctive African working-class leisure culture' (Ambler 1992: 348). In Roan, Epstein (1958: 10) observed how men and women met right next to elders discussing tribal issues and the gossiping of the urban elite. The beer hall fused the material and social aspects of rural life with the centralization of both alcohol and its ethnically diverse consumers in an urban setting. Township residents had their own ideas about how beer was to be consumed. Spearpoint recalled the following episode of 'natives' complaining about the spatial order of the company's beer hall:

I have had natives state that, as the drinking of beer is a friendly and social function, it is distasteful and unnatural to have to consume their beer in the presence, and very close proximity, of people with whom they have perhaps had a row or fight, or, in some instances, people of some tribe with whom they are not too friendly. (Spearpoint 1937: 31–32)

The company reacted by compartmentalizing the beer hall. Different types of rondavel were constructed. Epstein (1958: plate II) found brick-walled and reed-thatched ones in Roan, and I myself saw the remains of brick-walled round benches with metal umbrellas above and reed-thatched rondavels in Mpatamatu (see Figure 4.1).[4] However, the accommodation of people's ideas did not prevent individual and collective social unrest breaking out in the beer halls.[5] Furthermore, decentralized 'illicit' home brewing continually challenged the centralized provision of alcohol. Ambler (1992: 345–46) argues that mining companies never managed to control the drinking practices of their African labour force. His claim can be substantiated with research on the diverse economic practices of women, including beer brewing, in mine townships that I elaborated in Chapter 2.

Collings and Schaerer's development plan for Mpatamatu included the provision of 'Beer Halls' in the 'overall requirements' (RACM 1957: 4). The 'main Beer Garden', later to be called Kansengu Tavern, was opened in September 1962 and sited just opposite section 22 in the centre of the eastern part of Mpatamatu (see Map 0.1).[6] Both 'native beer', that is, *chibuku*, and bottled beer were sold (RST Roan Antelope Division 1964d: 1). Apparently the centralized provision of alcohol at one beer hall as noted by Wilson and observed by Epstein was abandoned by RACM. Mpatamatu was to receive several taverns spread among its sections. They were located on spacious plots and built with the mine houses around them. These conditions showed that they were planned as locations with a wider social function for the township residents. The social aspect, in fact, survived the abandonment of the taverns by the mine. This was illustrated to me by the group of men sharing a bottle of *chibuku* above. In the following passages, I revisit Mpatamatu's four surviving taverns.

Boniface Mwanza, a former sampling supervisor at the Geological Department of Zambia Consolidated Copper Mines' (ZCCM) Luanshya Division, first introduced me to Mpatamatu's social welfare buildings in April 2016. On a tour with him,[7] we looked for Kansengu Tavern's sitting tenant. Felix Matobwe lived in one of the former mine houses in section 24. He had been a mineworker since 1976, labouring underground at the 28th and Baluba shaft. In 2015, he retired from CNMC Luanshya Copper Mines (CLM). He showed us around the tavern.[8]

Kansengu Tavern was in a desolate state, ruined by time and climate, and broken by ransacking. However, the name sign had been freshly painted. In contrast to the few people around, there was a strong stench of alcohol. Walking through the dim light of the main room, past broken furniture towards the sales lady at the counter offering *chibuku*, I got to know the tavern as a broken relic of the mine's provisions for its workers. Felix Matobwe explained to me that he rented out parts of the building. Rather than generating an income, this was an attempt to stop the looting of the building after business hours. Ransacking

Figure 4.1. Kansumbi Tavern in section 25. Photo by the author.

had become a way to appropriate the material remains of the mine's welfare infrastructure in the township. Taverns were in a similar situation to government schools (see Chapter 3). 'If only the government could reopen 28th shaft, people are suffering a lot', Felix Matobwe exclaimed. The shaft had been Mpatamatu's raison-d'être. Felix Matobwe called for paternalist state intervention, in words referring to the time when the mine was run by a state-owned company. However, the period of ZCCM and government intervention was over. Luanshya's mayor, Nathan Chanda, redirected the call to reopen the 28th shaft to CLM (*Lusaka Times* 2017).

Kabulangeti Tavern, Mpatamatu's second beer hall, was built in section 23, also in 1962.[9] It was placed at a critical junction central to sections 22, 23 and 24 (see Map 0.1). In contrast to Kansengu Tavern, its tenant decided to break with the building's initial function as a bar by turning the beer hall into a church, a reappropriation I deal with later in this chapter.

Kansumbi Tavern, the township's third beer hall, was built off-centre, at the edge of the township between sections 24 and 25. It became operational in 1966.[10] The building looked abandoned but well maintained (see Figure 4.1), and, as I figured out over time, it was run as an outpost by its manager, Alfred Phiri. He had been born into a mineworker's family in Roan in 1951 and joined Roan Consolidated Mines (RCM) in the early 1970s. In 1999 he became the sitting tenant of Kansumbi Tavern. At that time, he was still employed by Roan Antelope Mining Corporation of Zambia (RAMCOZ). After being retrenched in 2004, he refocused on his tavern business. In 1998 he started another bar located more centrally in section 23. Alfred Phiri asked me to meet him there in his main office. This fact underlined the peripheral position of Kansumbi Tavern, a business that could not be run on its own and was only kept alive because it was subsidized by the success of the more centrally located bar.[11]

Mwaiseni Tavern, Mpatamatu's fourth beer hall, was built in the very east of the township, between section 22 and the former mine police compound (see Map 0.1). During my visits, I observed a lively place with men sipping beer on the veranda, music playing, and freshly erected election posters greeting me from the walls. However, I could not study the tavern's situation in detail, as the sitting tenant was seriously ill throughout my fieldwork.[12]

This brief history of Mpatamatu's four taverns reveals three issues that connected them with one another and with other social welfare buildings in the township. Firstly, the taverns were constructed in the eastern sections of the township before the 1970s. They therefore belonged to that part of Mpatamatu that had been developed during the height of corporate paternalism after the Second World War. The taverns were part of the more elaborate spatial order in sections 21 to 24 that housed many more social welfare buildings than sections 25 to 27 (see Chapter 1). Secondly, corporate paternalism made it possible to build social welfare buildings in peripheral locations because the mine township represented a material and social unit. A comprehensive corporate social investment plan made it possible to run them without a direct profit. As independent businesses, one of the taverns struggled with its disadvantageous location. Thirdly, their abandonment by the mine and the low purchasing power of Mpatamatu's population led the sitting tenants to reappropriate their taverns in different ways. Some struggled with rent and maintenance, others with low profits. At the same time, new bars were started, as in the case of the section 25 canteen, a former mine-run grocery store.[13]

RACM did not only build taverns in Mpatamatu to provide corporate spaces for alcohol consumption. As labour hierarchies spilled over into social life, mining companies also discovered that beer-drinking locations enabled them to 'divide and conquer', a corporate practice also pursued in the face of unionization (Larmer 2007: 36). Ambler (1992: 352–53) reconstructed how mining companies drew the class line between the taverns for ordinary mineworkers and the clubs for semi-skilled and skilled mineworkers. In Mpatamatu, the Buseko Recreation Club was one result of this process, a material analogue to class formation at the mines. 'Welfare Halls (i.e. social clubs)' had been listed next to 'Beer Halls' under the 'overall requirements' for the township by Collings and Schaerer (RACM 1957: 4).

Buseko Recreation Club was officially opened by RACM's African Personnel Officer in June 1962.[14] It was a tavern with additional facilities such as a lounge, theatre hall and offices. Only bottled beer was sold in the beginning (Mulenga Associates 1986b; RST Roan Antelope Division 1964a). This sales strategy emphasized the company's intention to separate ordinary mineworkers from 'advancees' who could afford to purchase bottled beer. Harries-Jones (1975: 163) had observed this corporate practice in neighbouring Roan earlier. European-type beer sold in bottles became a 'mark of status' (Ambler 1992: 353), the absence of which the committee member mentioned at the beginning of this chapter wanted to draw my attention to.

Kalulu Recreation Club,[15] Mpatamatu's second club, was established when the mine took over a private bar and restaurant from an Indian businessman in the market area of Mpatamatu in the course of the copper sector's nationalization in 1969/1970. The club was run in the same way as Buseko, relating class-based spaces of leisure to the distribution of allowances in kind to mineworkers. This distribution mainly involved mealie meal, as the club's former manager and accountant explained to me.[16] After ZCCM's privatization, one of the club's board members became the sitting tenant. Emmanuel Muyutu, a former mineworker under RCM, ZCCM and RAMCOZ, continued running Kalulu as a club and more than just a tavern. He employed four people, sold bottled beer and offered a pool table and darts to his customers.[17]

Fifty years after Buseko and Kalulu had been started as mine clubs, the committee member in conversation with me in front of Buseko returned to the question I have already touched upon in my short history of the township taverns: was it possible to run the clubs without the mine? This question had emerged in the 'Row over Roan clubs' books' in 1966 (*Mail Reporter* 1966). When the clubs' management had gradually been handed over to Africans during the early 1960s, the mine clubs turned into symbols of African self-management.

Africans opposed the corporate practice of interfering on the mine's behalf in times of financial difficulties. However, the clubs always relied on the financial support of the mine, just like the mineworkers themselves, explained the Buseko committee member. Certainly, '[the] company's primary business was to produce and sell copper at a profit', as Roan Selection Trust's (RST) General Manager noted during the club crisis in the late 1960s (RST Roan Antelope Division 1966a). At the same time, taverns and clubs needed to be maintained by the corporation as an integral part of the mine's unitary structure. After ZCCM's privatization, each tavern and club fell out of this structure and had to struggle for itself. Corporate abandonment and a grim economic outlook resulted in continuities and discontinuities in how particular buildings were run. Most importantly, beer halls were now run for a living by individuals, and not as a leisure service provided for by the mining company.

Miners Playing

As a mining town, Luanshya was renowned for its extensive sports facilities. First and foremost, it was known for the Roan Antelope Recreational Club (RARC) in the European mine township (see 'A' in Map 1.1). A swimming pool and a stadium were also built in the African mine township Roan. Football became the most popular game among African mineworkers.[18] Collings and Schaerer included a 'sports field' in their plans for Mpatamatu, proposing to build the township's stadium at the intersection of the administrative centre (market area), 'precinct 3' (later sections 23 and 24) and 'precinct 4' (later section 26; see Map 0.1) (RACM 1957: 1, appendix map NR.RA1).

After the first sections were built in the late 1950s, Collings and Schaerer worked out the details for the layout of the stadium in 1962. Construction work began at the end of the same year (RACM 1962: 1).

> We have been given no indication of what playing fields will be required as the central feature but, for the purposes of levelling and grassing, the plan indicates a rectangle 550 feet by 300 feet which will accommodate a standard international soccer pitch or a standard rugby ground and, in addition, athletic tracks and other athletic sports.
>
> The rectangle is oriented with the long axis 10° East of true North so as to avoid to the maximum players looking into the sun, and to take advantage of topography. The main spectators stand would be on the Western side facing East. (Collings & Schaerer Town Planning Consultants Consulting Engineers 1962: 1)

The layout plan revealed how Collings and Schaerer accommodated their design to the site's physical conditions, corporate prescriptions on the variety of disciplines, and the acceptance of specific games by the population of RACM's first African mine township. The popularity of football most probably induced

Figure 4.2. Mpatamatu stadium. Photo by the author.

the mining company to commission 'a standard international soccer pitch' and a 'spectators' stand' for Mpatamatu (see Figure 4.2). Following the supervision of alcohol consumption at taverns and clubs, the stadium as a place of after-work leisure reinforced the mine's spatial and temporal orders. Sport was permitted in an organized form *at* the stadium *after* work. As such, the stadium became the place for what van Onselen (1976: 191) termed 'organised sport', this being 'an important dimension of colonial hegemony':

> Colonial officials, European capitalists, and missionaries viewed orga-nized sports – football, cricket, field hockey, rugby – and the rules that characterized them as an important dimension of colonial hegemony. They believed that structured 'play' with rules and in a time framework inculcated time consciousness, discipline, courage, and endurance in Af-ricans. It fit into capitalist and Protestant notions of 'purposeful leisure', and redirected Africans from 'corrupting' leisure activities such as danc-ing and idle gossip. (Akyeampong and Ambler 2002: 11)

'Structured "play"' was taken up as a corporate practice, a corporate 'weapon in the control of large numbers of [Black] workers' (Onselen 1976: 191). Sport

became part of 'other forms of surveillance, control and command over bodies', which Victoria (2016: 256) saw in Foucauldian notions of architecture, a material environment that permitted 'internal, articulated and detailed control' (Foucault 1995: 172). In this sense, sports facilities joined mine houses, mine clinics, community centres, taverns and clubs as material locations envisaged as guaranteeing the controlled social reproduction of the labour force. However, the stadium also joined beer halls in its ability to assemble and mobilize people against the labour regime.[19]

After Zambia's independence in 1964 and the nationalization of the mines in 1969/1970, corporate sports facilities acquired national importance. Sports, particularly football, were upgraded from leisure activities for the mine's labour force to crucial activities of a newly independent nation state. Zambia's first president, Kenneth Kaunda, promoted football on a national scale (Chipande 2016: 62), building on earlier practices of corporate paternalism, such as sponsoring a football team at each mine. More than half of the eighteen players in Zambia's most famous national team had played for mine football clubs.[20] This state focus on sport reached its height under ZCCM, as the parastatal's guidelines on sport illustrate:

> ZCCM as a single major parastatal organisation should be geared to take the lead in the promotion of sport in compliance with the aims and objectives of the Party and its Government. (ZCCM 1984: 1)

In the shadow of the more successful Roan United Football Club in the neighbouring township, Mpatamatu stadium became the home of a succession of clubs supported by the mine: Buseko Rising Stars under ZCCM, Panado Football Club under RAMCOZ and Luanshya Copper Mines (LCM), and Nkulumashiba Football Club under CLM. However, support for a mine football club gradually declined after ZCCM's privatization. In 2012, Mpatamatu United Football Club was founded as an independent club. According to its secretary,[21] the team's ascent into the higher football divisions was hindered by the club's financial situation. In particular, transportation costs to away games posed a huge challenge in a vast country with a limited road network. Despite this situation, the club ran three youth teams, U13, U17 and U20, and held regular training sessions in a stadium that had become a beaten field of dry grass and dust (see Figure 4.2).

The construction of the sports complex east of the stadium during the second half of the 1980s further documented the 'promotion of sport' by ZCCM, which was backed by President Kaunda. Chrispin Mukapile, a former bricklayer in the maintenance section under RCM and ZCCM, explained to me how he became involved in making the final touches to the complex.[22] At the same time, Wisdom Zulu, who had just joined the Civil Engineering Department, was sent on a training course at the construction site shortly before its completion and commissioning in 1991.[23]

The Mpatamatu sports complex consisted of a central hall and two adjacent wings (see Figure 4.3). The hall was used for regular indoor sporting activities, such as chess, badminton and volleyball. The wings housed training rooms for boxers and weightlifters. Looking back at all those opportunities from today's dearth of sporting activities, one Mpatamatu resident exclaimed nostalgically: 'It was a very nice complex; everything was there'.[24]

Mpatamatu's residents engaged in sports at the stadium and the complex, and clubs and community centres housed additional indoor facilities. Hall B, a building south of and belonging to Buseko Club, became a training centre for boxing.[25] The 'promotion of sport' was all-encompassing and permitted such extraordinary expenses as a pitch irrigation scheme at the stadium.[26] Like other industrial contexts with enterprises with a unitary structure, sport was 'an important tool that could capture people in their free time and prevent them from being idle' (Starc 2010: 264). Cheering at or playing for one's mine team also enforced corporate identity and became a vehicle for motivation. Mining companies were inclined to invest in their football teams. One Luanshya resident who had worked at the mine for over thirty years recalled:

> Management knew that there was a relationship between production and social activities, . . . every time the weekend results [of Roan United Football Club] were bad, production on Monday and Tuesday was lower.[27]

Felix Chanda grew up during that era of the 'promotion of sport' and had spent a lot of time at Mpatamatu's stadium. He had been born in Muchinga Province and had grown up in the township from 1989 to 1996. Living with one of his maternal aunt's daughters in section 23, he became a registered de-

Figure 4.3. Mpatamatu's former sports complex. Photo by the author.

pendant of his cousin's mineworker husband. This dependence fully integrated him into the mine's unitary structure. He went to Mpatamatu Primary School and enjoyed access to the township's sports facilities. In his survey, Mijere (1985: 301–2) showed that the great majority of mine township residents under ZCCM's Luanshya Division were aware of these opportunities for their children and took advantage of them.

At secondary school, Felix Chanda got involved in athletics and regularly trained at the stadium: 'Everything was looking nice, the stadium was green, there was football, volleyball, handball and athletics'. Long jump and high jump became his disciplines, and he competed in tournaments in other Copperbelt towns. 'It used to be a very exciting time for us youths, this going outside in sports attire, so beautiful.'[28] Sport not only provided after-school activities for children, it connected pupils and their mineworker families with others inside and outside the copper sector through inter-divisional tournaments, that is, within ZCCM, and inter-provincial ones, that is, within the Ministry of Education.

Felix Chanda remembered such events, like the 1992 Inter-provincial Athletics Championship for Secondary Schools and the ZCCM Youth Cross Country Championship held at the Kafubu (Roan township) and Mpatamatu stadiums, events I found documented in the archives (Copperbelt Basic and Secondary Schools Heads' Association 1992; ZCCM 1992). The tournaments connected the township and its residents like Felix Chanda to the outside world. This connection was lost when the mine abandoned the social welfare buildings.

I was able to observe how the stadium was used as meeting place, as well as being the training ground for the local football club. One September day in 2016, I walked across the Nkulumashiba Stream towards section 26 with four women, who were returning home from a farmers' cooperative gathering. They had just attended a meeting with a Seed Co representative and had been instructed in the use of a new maize seed and the application of pesticides.[29] Agriculture was seen as an important alternative to the formal sector in post-paternalist times. Symbolically, farm plots were gradually encroaching on the barren sports field, with its decaying stand, from the west, while the complex building shielded it from vegetable gardens approaching it from the central roundabout to the east.

At the complex, music was another kind of 'purposeful leisure' that mineworkers were encouraged to engage in after work. Each of ZCCM's divisions had financed a mine band. Several former mineworkers told me how Luanshya Division's band rehearsed at the complex in Mpatamatu. Outside bands played exclusively for miners. Ticket costs were deducted directly from mineworkers' pay cheques. Wisdom Zulu remembered the 1991 music competition of the Department of Cultural Services of the Copperbelt Province at the complex, which featured bands from Luanshya, Ndola, Kitwe, Mufulira and Chililabombwe.[30] In the past, several township residents confirmed, famous Congolese musicians such as Pépé Kallé and Bozi Boziana had toured the Copperbelt mine towns.

During my fieldwork, this musical past revisited Mpatamatu's sports complex. The building still possessed the capacity to assemble people, and it had kept its stage. The Mpatamatu College of Education (MPACE) student union organized a fund-raising concert, booking popular Zambian artists and organizing security, expecting about five hundred people to come. Interestingly, in conversation with the organizers of a younger generation, it became clear that the complex was perceived as a house of prayer, detached from its past as a concert hall under the mines. The students' greatest concern was that the building '[was] a church [and that] immoral things are not supposed to happen'.[31] The union representatives made it clear that their goal was to raise awareness of education. 'People cannot invest in education but they can invest in beer', exclaimed one of the representatives, referring to the cheap *chibuku* being drunk everywhere in the township. Instead, the concert would give township residents the option to spend their money on a ticket to support MPACE's union.

Nostalgia for Infrastructure

The material remains of social settings produced by corporate paternalism that I have described in this chapter, namely socializing at a tavern or club, doing athletics at the stadium or holding a concert at the complex, generated a strong sense of nostalgia for the days of ZCCM and its post- and pre-independence predecessors, RCM, RST and RACM. Several Copperbelt scholars have noted the resilience of nostalgia in the former mining towns.[32] Facing the ruinous consequences of corporate abandonment, nostalgia on the Copperbelt was aimed at 'a golden age of corporate paternalism' (Larmer and Laterza 2017: 702). On the Copperbelt too, nostalgia followed a watershed (Boym 2001: xvi), namely the reprivatization of the Zambian copper sector in 1997. In the case of Mpatamatu, the nostalgia was particularly for the infrastructures of that past 'golden age'.

Following Mususa's (2014: 79) reading of Casey (1987: 379) and Mah's (2008: 237–38) reading of Harper (1966: 120), I understand nostalgia as something intrinsically ambiguous. In Mpatamatu I encountered this ambiguity in the presence of broken infrastructures from a modern past, the affects triggered by their brokenness, the positive assessment of opportunities provided by corporate paternalism, and the neglect of the fact that welfare buildings also represented a tool of social control. 'Warm memories' blurred the rigidity of mine township life, as observed by Finn (1998: 108) at Anaconda Copper Mining Company in Chile. Larmer and Laterza (2017: 702) rightly underline the fact that the Copperbelt 'company towns were . . . sites primarily designed to control and discipline labour'. However, what I saw residents associate with Mpatamatu under corporate paternalism most frequently was not limitation or even control, but opportunity.

Nostalgia in Mpatamatu revolved around a socially inscribed materiality, for example the mine club as a place of social status and economic privilege, and it curved both space and time by, for example, relating social situations of the past to the ruined spaces of the present. In conversation with my research participants, how things were before they had fallen apart was immediately present in the face of the material ruination of the township's infrastructures. 'How things were' always included residents' past social lives and material living environments. In the most literal sense of the term – a longing, Greek *álgos*, for coming home, *nostos* (Boym 2001: xv–xvi) – I witnessed moments of nostalgia during fieldwork in Mpatamatu.

Residents longed for the opportunities that had been provided by the mine township and its infrastructures, which had constituted their living environment under corporate paternalism. Affects about present conditions were always put up against that past. Clearly residents saw progress in the infrastructures that the subsequent mining companies had put in place since the beginning of industrial copper mining in Luanshya in the late 1920s. When I talked to them and thought with them about what was left, this 'progress still controlled us even in tales of ruination' (Tsing 2015: 21).

What was left were pot-holed streets under broken street lamps, mine houses without electricity and running water, and social welfare buildings disconnected from the corporate structure. In their dysfunction, infrastructures produced a longing for its initial creators. Corporate abandonment invited in the spectre of the imperial formations that had once turned the Copperbelt into an 'extractive space' (Frederiksen 2010: 236–41) through 'imperial nostalgia' (Stoler 2008b: 199). Nostalgia for infrastructure was common in postcolonial spaces where governments could not maintain it and where people, in the face of material ruination, reverted to 'value the roads, hospitals, and schools built during the colonial era' (Piot 1999: 43). Nostalgia for infrastructure in Mpatamatu was very concrete: it was not aimed, in contrast to other places, at an unfulfilled vision of streets, houses and social welfare buildings (cf. Yarrow 2017).

This concreteness was formulated selectively relative to residents' personal experiences made under corporate paternalism in the past and the corporate abandonment of the present. A former mine football player raved about the pitch irrigation scheme at Mpatamatu stadium under ZCCM; a former boxing trainer highlighted the numerous facilities where he used to train adolescents; a former homecraft teacher complained about the women not learning at the community centres but drinking in bars; and a teacher who went to pre-school and enjoyed sports activities after school at the community centres emphasized the utilitarian character of the former social welfare buildings.

Miners Praying

In contrast to nostalgia for the social welfare buildings as locations of opportunity, analytically, they suggested themselves to be an effigy of Foucault's notion of power as a 'total structure of actions brought to bear upon possible actions' (Foucault 1982: 789). Indeed, community centres, taverns, clubs, clinics, the stadium and the sports complex structured the behaviour of the mine township residents. They incited women to take up homecraft classes and promoted the gendered division of labour. They invited men to go for an after-work beer at a particular location and directed youths to the sports facilities after school. The scope for action of a mine township resident was predefined: it was impossible to evade the unitary structure of the mine entirely. However, there was one space not under the immediate authority of the mine that residents were drawn into: religion.

In a survey carried out at ZCCM's Nkana, now part of Mopani Copper Mines (MCM), and Luanshya Division during his fieldwork from 1982 to 1983, Mijere found something that kept township residents out of the mine's leisure facilities: more than half of his interlocutors indicated that 'they were not interested in beer or sports. They . . . would, instead, go to church to pray and to involve themselves in church activities' (Mijere 1985: 298–99). One of his sources revealed that he could not be a member of a club where beer was served while at the same time being a member of the church. The mineworkers Mijere included in his survey were of an older generation, in their late forties, having been born in the early 1930s. In contrast, the younger mineworkers in the survey did make use of the leisure facilities. My point here is not that there was a correlation between age and the effectiveness of corporate control through welfare buildings. Rather, the church represented a concrete alternative to corporate provision aimed at the life of the labour force outside the mine shaft.

The almost exclusionary character of the choice between corporate leisure provision such as socializing at a beer hall and involvement in church activities, as indicated by one of Mijere's sources above, was also present in my own biographical interviews with Mpatamatu's residents. In every conversation about the former social welfare buildings, I sought to enquire how frequently residents in fact visited them. As a pattern, taverns and clubs appeared as counterparts to churches. Interestingly, these different social spheres played a role when social welfare buildings were reappropriated as houses of prayer. The past of the buildings would be put to use in the present of the churches.

Kabulangeti Tavern had attracted my attention ever since I passed the junction in section 23 at which it was located for the first time (see Map 0.1). The building carried obvious marks of material ruination and renovation. An incomplete brick-walled annex stood next to the original structure (see Figure 4.4). The name of the former beer hall was nowhere to be found. Instead, the name of a congregation and academy, a pre-school, as I later found out, was painted on its outer walls. The large plot around the building was undeveloped, the grass having been trampled down along the footpaths. A tall tree made me think of mineworkers formerly sitting in its shade sipping their after-work beer. The building seemed abandoned, depicting a sharp contrast with Mpatamatu's 'flats' on the

Figure 4.4. Former Kabulangeti Tavern in section 23. Photo by the author.

other side of the road, which were the source of much noise of life: children screaming, pots clattering, chickens clucking.[33]

The sitting tenant, Steven Mulenga, had struggled for several years to continue running Kabulangeti Tavern as a beer hall. It appeared to be an ill-fated endeavour right from the start. The building had been stripped of its heart, the beer tank, by a former tenant. Turning the interior into classrooms for a pre-school project also failed: the Moraiah Academy had to close because of a lack of funds. In conversation he recalled the year 2013, when he 'surrendered the building to God'.[34] Steven Mulenga had been a mineworker himself in various ZCCM divisions from 1988 to 1991. In his last post he worked as an electrician. The skills he acquired enabled him to start his own car repair business. In 2001 he moved from Luanshya's Mikomfwa township to Mpatamatu. In 2007 he started to lease out Kabulangeti Tavern from RAMCOZ in receivership.

Steven Mulenga needed a preacher to turn the former tavern into a house of prayer. His wife Agness supported him. She had joined the Dynamic Worship Church International (DWCI) and had taken Bible classes. DWCI was a Pentecostal congregation based in Lusaka. Agness Mulenga held the first service in December 2013. They started with a group of five adults and three children, she recalled. Over time, church attendance increased to about fifty people. However, Agness Mulenga admitted that attendance was directly linked to her presence and that she could not preach every Sunday. Consequently, numbers had fallen again.

At the tavern, Steven Mulenga showed me how they had converted the beer hall into a 'Hall of God' (see Figure 4.5).[35] The dance floor in front of the counter had become his wife's workplace. Armchairs were arranged for her and the church elders. Separated by concrete pillars, the congregation sat, stood, knelt, sung and prayed in the former beer lounge. The kitchen behind the counter remained unused and had been covered with decorative veils, a background to the speaker's desk in the centre of the room. The disco illumination and a metal cage for a stereo had been left on the walls. School benches in the main room and letter

Figure 4.5. The prayer room in former Kabulangeti Tavern. Photo by the author.

sheets on the pillars were the remaining traces of Steven Mulenga's pre-school project. A door to the west led into another former classroom that appeared to be used as a store. The door next to the counter opened into a kitchen and store, an office, the old beer tank storage room and the former take-away kiosk (Mulenga Associates 1986a). From the kiosk we entered the unfinished brick-walled annex that I had already seen from the outside (Figure 4.4). The former beer hall had not only been turned into a prayer house: Steven and Agness Mulenga intended to move into the extended structure themselves. Their plan was to save the money that was currently going on rent for another house in Mpatamatu.

I arrived early one Sunday morning. The building was locked, and no one was present at the time that had been communicated to me. Waiting, I sensed the township morning: rooster cries, fires crackling, music playing. Patriotic Front (PF) campaign cars were driving down Kalulu Street, as the general election was less than a month away. A woman street trader shouted out the vegetables she had for sale. A man with the letters 'CLM' on his shirt passed by. Children giggled at me from afar. People were on the move, some riding bicycles, presumably to the church of their choice. After about an hour, three young men arrived and opened the door. I sat down in the main room on one of the benches. A woman with her baby boy joined me. Eventually, one of the three men started the service. Agness Mulenga arrived later, by which time about twenty people were present, but she left the day's sermon to one of her junior pastors.[36]

How much the memory of the place mattered occurred to me during one of Agness Mulenga's own sermons. Standing at the centre of the former beer hall, she referred to the building's past as a place of drinking. The tavern became a metaphor for the presence of evil and deliverance from it. Brochures of the US-American child evangelization ministry 'Mailbox Club' describing the origins of the devil were displayed on the benches, directing every last bit of attention to the topic. Basing her sermon on the temptation of Christ, as detailed in Matthew 4:1–11, Agness Mulenga evoked the cleansing of the building:

The devil is in the mind of the people. . . . This was a place of drinking
and HIV. . . . We answered God's call and are destroying the evil. The
day of judgement will come. You are going to be judged, if you want it
or not.[37]

The leisure activities of drinking and dancing in the past were thus rendered sin-
ful as manifestations of the devil. The material ruination of the tavern appeared
to mirror the destruction of evil. At the same time, the tidiness and decoration
of the prayer room indicated the congregation's urge to answer God's call. Again,
amidst ruination there was renovation: although sections of the building were
falling apart, others were being renovated. The building's surroundings were
covered with rubbish blown over the dry grass by the wind, the walls of the
prayer room had been freshly painted, and construction work was going on.
Renovation also consisted in the fragmented processes of trying to make a living
at the former beer hall: from a mineworker who became a car mechanic and tavern manager to his wife studying to preach and making her husband the verger
of her church.

A few minutes by foot along Kalulu Street, the Mpatamatu sports complex was the most prominent example of a former leisure facility being converted into a house of prayer. Pastor Anthony Kabwe remembered that it was
in December 1999 when his congregation of the Pentecostal Assemblies of
God (Zambia) (PAOG(Z)) first used the main hall of the complex for Sunday
services.[38] Formed between 1955 and 1970, PAOG(Z) was an offspring of the
Pentecostal Assemblies of Canada (PAOC), a Pentecostal movement that had
been brought to Zambia by Canadian missionaries. PAOC had been part of
the first Pentecostal wave going back to the Azusa Street Revival at the beginning of the twentieth century.[39] Pastor Kabwe had been raised as a Catholic,
but became a 'born again' Pentecostal in 1979. After attending a Bible college
for three years, he was first posted to Mufulira before coming to Mpatamatu
in 1996.

Pastor Kabwe remembered that the situation in the neighbourhood of the
complex was a challenge to the church in the early 2000s. Bars had mushroomed
in the abandoned wings of the building. In order to emphasize its claim to the
complex, the church signed a rental agreement with RAMCOZ in receivership,
making PAOG(Z) the main sitting tenant. Over the years, the building was repeatedly put up for sale. A 2013 sales advertisement was the last so far of many
unsuccessful attempts by the receiver to turn the mine's social assets into cash
(RAMCOZ (in receivership) 2013).

After the bars had left the complex, other groups continued to use the building's wings. Apparently, a martial arts group was active there in the 2000s. At
the time of my fieldwork, four of the five rooms in the wings were being used as
extension classrooms of Nzelu Zanga Private School, a school founded in 2002,

explained the headteacher, Mercy Tembo, to me in the main building of the school across from the complex.[40] The fifth room was the only relict of the complex's original intent, still being a part-time gym for weightlifters.

The main hall of the complex was adapted to PAOG(Z)'s requirements, being used as a house of prayer with an ancillary school. In 2007, the congregation started Victoria's Christian Private School. This primary school grew to about two hundred pupils and eight teachers. It was envisaged as offering education to the community and thus supplementing the congregation's funds. Two rectangular classrooms were created by putting up wooden boards to the left and to the right of the main entrance (see Figure 4.6). Like the situation in the former pay line buildings, smaller classrooms were carved out of a larger space. The school turned out to be a 'charitable organization', confessed Pastor Kabwe. Like other private schools in Mpatamatu, the rate of payment of school fees was very low, resulting in a high turnover of both pupils and teachers.[41]

Charitable organizations had been developed at other former social welfare buildings in Mpatamatu as well. The former section 21 clinic became the headquarters of the Serve Zambia Foundation. This non-governmental organization (NGO) had been started as a faith-based health care service by Pastor Andrew Kayekesi in 1997. When the mine clinics in Mpatamatu deteriorated after ZCCM's privatization, health care for the people in the rural areas next to the township became a serious problem. The pastor started a home-based care programme in the Mpata Hills. At the time of my fieldwork, the Serve Zambia Foundation was focused on helping child-headed homes and fighting HIV/AIDS. Its work was supported by a global network of different faith-based organizations.[42]

Sunday services in the main hall of the complex drew between fifty and a hundred people. According to Pastor Kabwe, members of the community were very heterogeneous with regard to their occupational backgrounds. Nowadays there were few miners, many having turned to subsistence farming in order to

Figure 4.6. The main hall of Mpatamatu's former sports complex. Photo by the author.

make a living. Services usually began with music audible from far away and were started by a junior pastor. A growing number of people gradually arrived at the complex. On stage, singing with a band and choir alternated with collective and individual prayers. The zeal and exertions of the junior pastor and the centrality of the music during the service were reminiscent of the building's former use as a gymnasium and concert hall.

About one hour into the service, Pastor Kabwe climbed onto the stage. His sermon, permeated with Bible readings and references, usually took one to one and a half hours. Offerings, typical of the prosperity gospel, were made (Haynes 2017: 68). Finally, community announcements closed the service.[43] I observed this roughly three-hour routine at all the Pentecostal congregations that were convened in Mpatamatu's former social welfare buildings. However, PAOG(Z) was the only one where I witnessed Holy Communion. It was also the largest Pentecostal assembly with the most resources, with benches, stage equipment, instruments, a sound system and a substantial number of followers.

Apart from the recurring intense performances by the pastors, physical exertion played a minor role at the complex during the time of my fieldwork. The sports complex had lost its attributed function within the broader corporate social theme. Again, a former social welfare building had been abandoned and had to stand by itself. It was reassessed through its material characteristics like the tall church-like outer walls, the high widespread roof and the ground beneath allowing numerous people to gather there. The complex remained the single largest hall in the township, surpassing the capacity of the Catholic Church, the United Church of Zambia (UCZ), the numerous Kingdom Halls of Jehovah's Witnesses and the other newly constructed Pentecostal churches in Mpatamatu. For its main sitting tenant, the building's material characteristics and location far outstripped its run-down condition.

Miners Preaching

Former social welfare buildings were thus reappropriated as churches. Moreover, former mineworkers became preachers themselves. In my investigation into the buildings' post-paternalist history, I encountered two ministries that used them for Sunday services and that were headed by miners-turned-pastors. Their congregations were relatively small, not comparable to the size of PAOG(Z)'s Mpatamatu branch, but rather that of DWCI at the former Kabulangeti Tavern. One congregation rented out a classroom from the Suzika Private School at the pay line buildings, the other a classroom at the Golden Eagle Private School in the former Muliashi Community Centre (see Chapter 3). Both cases exemplify how the material products of corporate paternalism and its human subjects found a new purpose in Christianity after the disintegration of the mine's unitary structure.

Pastor Mukosha was born in Serenje District, Central Province, in 1958. He joined ZCCM's Nchanga Division, now part of Konkola Copper Mines (KCM), in 1985. His congregation, the House of Deliverance, had been started by a mineworker in Chingola in the early 1990s. According to Pastor Mukosha, the first members were all mineworkers. In 1992 he entered the congregation as a 'first child', one of its first members. Over the years, he rose in the church's hierarchy and ultimately started a new branch under his pastorship in Mpatamatu in 2007. Two years later, House of Deliverance moved to the former community centre.[44] His congregation was not alone: two other ministries used classrooms in the buildings belonging to it for their Sunday services as well.[45]

Mpatamatu's branch of House of Deliverance appeared to me to be a family church, as Sunday services not only involved Pastor Mukosha but also his wife and daughter. During the service I attended, his daughter delivered the main sermon. Pastor Mukosha sat down next to me on one of the school benches. We were among ten people, seven of them women, who followed his wife's singing and her instructions for prayer before the sermon.[46] From time to time, the songs and prayers of the ministry congregating across the building were audible. Like other services I attended, testimonies – oral evidence key to one's own Christian identity – were presented by followers in front of the congregation. One of the few men came forward. He talked about his nightly readings of the scriptures. Before he left, he underlined that 'it's our duty to tell God what we want' with the following reference:

Don't worry about anything, but pray about everything. With thankful hearts, offer up your prayers and requests to God. (Philippians 4:6)[47]

I was perplexed. It was far from the first time that I had come across Philippians 4:6 in Mpatamatu. I had initially picked it up at the home of Steven and Agness Mulenga, who, as we have seen, had turned Kabulangeti Tavern into a church. In their living room, TV3, Zambia National Broadcasting Corporation's Christian music channel, was running while we were talking. A singer chanted: 'You should not worry about tomorrow, you should not worry in your life, Jesus is your way!' In a second example, a junior pastor at the tavern-turned-church fell into a mantra repeating Philippians 4:6 again and again.[48] It also came up during one of PAOG(Z)'s Sunday services at the sports complex: the woman preaching ensured the community that 'you don't have to worry about tomorrow, you're a child of God!'[49]

In light of the prosperity gospel, 'Jesus . . . encouraged the believers to seek, knock, and ask (translated as *claim*)' (Kalu 2008: 258), the repeated appearance of Philippians 4:6 was not surprising. As someone who had examined the history of the former social welfare buildings, these instances possessed a historical quality for me. Certainly, churches had been active in the township since its inception. However, I came to understand Philippians 4:6 as a spiritual mirror image of the past corporate paternalism under which claims were addressed to the mining company.

Social welfare buildings might have been repurposed and mineworkers might have become preachers, yet a particular social logic did not cease to exist: '*being* someone continued to imply *belonging* to someone' (Ferguson 2013: 228). Ferguson (2013: 226) explored 'dependence' not as 'bondage or unfreedom', but as a 'hierarchical affiliation that created the most important forms of free choice'. Mineworkers could not build upon their affiliation with the mine any more, and the municipality had not managed to step in fully to replace it. More than ever, it was 'God's promised generosity' that provided people with a 'spiritual contract' they could rely on in times of material and social ruination (Kalu 2008: 255).

Pastor Mukosha's daughter made it clear what this spiritual contract meant to her. She preached on the story of the resuscitation of the Shunammite's son. 'God wants us to make impossible things possible', she shouted. Poverty originated with people's inability to listen to God. In fact, it was the devil who was to be avoided by sharing the little wealth one had. She assured the congregation that 'there [will be] a day of your harvest'.[50] In retrospect, and through the literature on Pentecostalism, I recognized her sermon as a prototype of the prosperity gospel, with its image of cultivating one's field, the centrality it gave to the faith doctrine and its equivalence of poverty with the devil (Attanasi 2012: 5; Kalu 2008: 255–56).

It was in Pastor Mukosha's church that I experienced a particularly rich instance of reflecting my own positionality and back story together with my research participants in the field. Through my mother's biography (see the Introduction), I related Mpatamatu to a post-paternalist community in the former German Democratic Republic: Schkopau. People were very interested in where I came from and why I had come to Mpatamatu in the first place. Why was I studying their township's history and its former social welfare buildings?

In a first reply, I retraced my fieldwork trajectory and explained my initial research interest in Chinese companies investing in Zambia's copper industry. People actively related to my experience of being kept out by the mine operators, alluding to the absence of corporate social responsibility measures in Mpatamatu. In a second reply, I talked about Buna and the ruinous consequences of the privatization of East Germany's economy after 1990. Entire industrial regions were downsized or dissolved. I explained how Buna's *Kulturhaus* was still an unused ruin today stuck in its own past. I talked about the high unemployment among former Buna employees. Despite the fact that I had grown up in a family of *Wendegewinner*, that is, 'winners' of German reunification, I was taught from an early age to look at the world from the perspective of the disconnected and marginalized. In this sense, I had come to Pastor Mukosha's church and service in order to listen and learn.

Pastor Mpundu was around the same age as Pastor Mukosha's daughter. He had been born into a mineworker's family living in Roan township. Like Pastor Kabwe of the PAOG(Z), he grew up in a Catholic household. During adolescence he became interested in the Pentecostal movement for both personal and doctrinal reasons. His father had worked for the maintenance department of ZCCM's Luanshya Division. He initially followed his father into plumbing, painting and plastering. After temporarily working as a mine police officer at Lumwana mine (now part of Barrick Gold, North-Western Province), he returned to Luanshya. In 2008 he started his own ministry in Mpatamatu, one year before being ordained by a US-American priest. Like House of Deliverance, Pastor Mpundu's congregation first rented out rooms in one of the former community centres. However, the rooms at Kansengu Community Centre were too small. Eventually he moved his ministry to the Suzika Private School at the former pay line buildings.

One Sunday morning in August 2016, I returned to Mpatamatu's pay line buildings in order to attend one of Pastor Mpundu's services. It was being held in one of the many classrooms that had been cut out of the long low halls where mineworkers used to receive their salaries (see Figure 3.1). It was a very bright and windy day, with dust from the open pit hanging over Mpatamatu. The Mpata Hills were hardly visible on the horizon beyond the township. Pastor Mpundu spotted me as I approached the door and invited me into his church. I entered the small dark room and experienced something like a compression of space, time and the spoken word. The service had already started, and I was drawn into a situation described best in the verses of the scripture itself:

When the day of Pentecost came, they were all together in one place. Suddenly a sound like the blowing of a violent wind came from heaven and filled the whole house where they were sitting. They saw what seemed to be tongues of fire that separated and came to rest on each of them. All of them were filled with the Holy Spirit and began to speak in other tongues as the Spirit enabled them. (Acts 2:1–4)

Despite the fact that only ten adults and four children were present in the room, the atmosphere resembled that in the scripture: shouts of deep personal prayer, voices reflected by the brick walls and being multiplied, utterances in English, Bemba and 'tongues', all floating in the room's heat descending onto the congregation from the metal roof plates above it. The day's central reading was the parable of 'The Rich Man and Lazarus' and the question of whether riches were bad for followers of Christ.[51] Everyone, including me, was asked to join the discussion, which was headed by a junior pastor. The lecture ended after about an hour with a combination of communal singing and personal prayers.[52]

By the time Pastor Mpundu started preaching himself, almost two hours into the service, the number of people present had doubled. Attendance was growing, as was the heat in the room. The pastor started a monologue on God enabling his people to act. He gradually lost his voice; his elaborations occasionally being accompanied by the congregation's 'Amen'. Towards the end of the service, the message 'Leave your troubles with the Lord' filled the room, a message I saw being related to the words of Philippians 4:6 noted above. After three and a half hours the service closed with hymns and community announcements.

Pastor Mpundu's ministry had been renting the room from the Suzika Private School in the pay line buildings since 2011, he told me when I visited him at his home.[53] We were sitting in the living room, where the Hillsong Channel was running on TV. At other homes in Mpatamatu, I repeatedly saw Emmanuel TV on screen. Both channels were internationally broadcast programmes by two major Pentecostal churches. The former was run by the Hillsong Church in Sydney, the Australian branch of the Assemblies of God, the latter by the Synagogue, Church of All Nations (SCOAN) in Lagos, a Pentecostal church headed by T.B. Joshua.

I witnessed how present SCOAN and its 'prophet' were in Mpatamatu during another service at Pastor Mpundu's church. A senior pastor, a guest of Pastor Mpundu, who had been with the ministry for almost thirty years, held the main sermon on another Sunday. His authority immediately filled the room, reducing the people in the audience, including myself, to students. His zeal became apparent when he started reading about 'winning souls':

Therefore go and make disciples of all nations, baptizing them in the name of the Father and of the Son and of the Holy Spirit, and teaching them to obey everything I have commanded you. And surely I am with you always, to the very end of the age. (Matthew 28:19–20)

The senior pastor continued with a forceful lecture on God's all-encompassing authority and the need of a vision for his followers. His words seemed almost intimidating: 'We [the pastors] are the final authority, this is a church of God not *yamuntu* [of man], this is not a club!' His words shattered the idea that the building had once been used to hand out money to mineworkers that they then spent on a beer at a club. Nothing escaped his presence as he disciplined two young men who were chatting with each other. He shouted: 'In T.B. Joshua's church there is order!' He underlined his call for discipline by citing the scripture again. The roughly twenty people and myself listened in silence.

Without guidance from God law and order disappear, but God blesses everyone who obeys his Law. (Proverbs 29:18)

Following the pastor's one-hour sermon, during which most people just nodded occasionally or replied to his statements with 'Amen', individual prayers refilled the room. Again, the service turned into a mixture of heat, cries, shouts and songs. A junior pastor took up the theme of the guest: 'Desire God to lead you in this world!'[54] Indeed, it was guidance people most often called out for in the services I attended during my fieldwork in Mpatamatu.

Global (Re-)Connect

Based on his work on urban social life on the Zambian Copperbelt, Ferguson (1999: 234–54; 2006: 48–9; 2009) argued repeatedly that mineworkers, like the country itself, had met the fate of a 'global disconnect' since the fall of the copper price in the 1970s. This disconnect unfolded in 'abjection', that is, the 'process of being thrown aside, expelled, or discarded' (Ferguson 1999: 236). He based his argument on a historical context in which Zambia first ascended to 'membership in the new world society' through national independence and was then gradually disconnected from it due to the declining price and importance of copper (Ferguson 1999: 239–43). ZCCM's privatization in 1997 formally reconnected Zambia's most important industrial sector with international capital. The economic involvement in the country of actors from the People's Republic of China (PRC) revived the demand for copper. However, this reconnection on the level of capital did not result in a reconnection on the local level. The reprivatization of Zambia's copper sector renewed the social abjection of the local.

The retrenchments in Luanshya in the early 2000s following RAMCOZ's bankruptcy expelled mineworkers and their dependants from the living environment that the mine had provided. Many were declared 'redundant', a term I found given as a reason in the RAMCOZ retrenchment lists that I studied and also found reflected in Bauman's (2008: 12) words on the outcasts of modernity. Mine operators retreated from the residential areas accommodating their labour force and the social welfare buildings within them. Looking at 'abjection' from Mpatamatu, I recognized its social and material aspects as going along with a process of post-paternalist ruination. Abjection explained the nostalgia for infrastructure, for being connected, as well as the claims put forward in the churches mentioned above.

Pentecostalism, and particularly the prosperity gospel, were a way for people in Mpatamatu to reconnect with the world and their own past modernity. PAOG(Z) apparently comprised 450 congregations in Zambia in 2000 (Chalwe 2008: 25), being connected with the global ministry of the Assemblies of God. TV sets connected the township's residents with global Pentecostal movements, and televangelists spoke to them in their living rooms. In buildings where mineworkers had reaffirmed themselves as belonging to the nation's most important labour segment and to an international copper community, people who were economically redundant claimed a place in a Christian world community. Membership in the world society was not linked to capital any more, but reconfirmed in religion articulated in a Christian faith:

> Our Father in heaven, help us to honour your name. Come and set up your kingdom, so that everyone on earth will obey you, as you are obeyed in heaven. Give us our food for today. Forgive us for doing wrong, as we forgive others. Keep us from being tempted and protect us from evil. (Matthew 6:9–13)[55]

Prayer replaced mine identification cards. As with Haynes' (2012: 135–36) field site in Kitwe, social bonds were created through membership in a Pentecostal church. Religion, not industry, became the social context in which people established themselves as 'relational persons', that is, as living in relations of dependence that created opportunities (Ferguson 2013: 226). In a former mine township like Mpatamatu this position of being related often involved the former social welfare buildings. In fact, the structures that had been put to new uses since the collapse of corporate paternalism established new connections within Mpatamatu, Zambia and beyond. This global (re-)connect revealed itself when Pastor Kabwe of the PAOG(Z) proclaimed in front of the community in Mpatamatu's former sports complex:

> You can be in China praying, in Japan praying . . . Jesus will hear you! . . . Speak out to God! . . . In your local language you can cry out![56]

Like the mineworkers and their families, the social welfare buildings had been abandoned by the mine. People and buildings both fell out of a unitary structure that had regulated their lives and connected them to the outside world. While the mine as a site of mineral extraction was reconnected to the world through capital, its townships as social extensions of this site of extraction were not. In this sense, buildings like the former sports complex represented both aspects of Ferguson's (2009: 325) notion of (dis-)connect: a site 'where the globalization of the economy has been experienced as disconnection and abjection', and a site where 'highly selective and spatially encapsulated forms of global connection' were re-established (Ferguson 2006: 14). The buildings' potency contained both the severing and connecting of relations against the background of their material state. However, the context of their ability to connect and how they connected people with the outside world had changed immensely since ZCCM's privatization.

Notes

1. *Chibuku* is an indigenous variety of beer made from different cereals. According to Richards (1969: footnote 2, 76), the Bemba, who historically had made up the largest part of the Copperbelt's workforce on the mines, preferred the type based on millet. The beer sold under the brand 'Kankoyo White Beer', which I observed being drunk in Mpatamatu, is based on sorghum and maize.
2. Buseko Recreation Club committee member, interview with the author, 13 May 2016, Mpatamatu.
3. Mususa (2010: 384; 2014: 213) had previously observed the relationship between social status and type of alcohol being drunk by Luanshya's residents.
4. Field notes by the author, 28 April 2016.
5. For instance the 1935 and 1963 strikes in Luanshya. See Whelan (1963: 4–5), Chauncey (1981: 146).
6. *Kansengu* referred to the 'large bamboos near Irwin [18th] shaft' across the main road from the tavern. See MMTMB (1961: 1; 1962: 2) and RACM (1957: 1, 5).
7. Boniface Mwanza, first township tour with the author, 28 April 2016, Mpatamatu.
8. Felix Matobwe, site inspection with the author, 28 April 2016, Mpatamatu.
9. See RST Roan Antelope Division (1962a). *Kabulangeti* is a 'corruption of the English word, "blanket" . . . [and] refers to the original [Basotho] shaft sinkers at MacLaren [28th] shaft' (MMTMB 1961: 1).
10. See RST Roan Antelope Division (1966b). *Kansumbi* is the name of a local stream. It also denotes rats and other small animals, *(a)ka*-, that are 'sniffed out', *-sumba*, by dogs. See MMTMB (1961: 1; 1965).
11. Alfred Masauso Phiri, interview with the author, 6 August 2016, Mpatamatu.
12. *Mwaiseni* is the Bemba word for 'welcome'. I only engaged in intensive on-site fieldwork after a visit together with the sitting tenant. Unfortunately, this initial introduction could not take place. Also, I could not find any documents related to Mwaiseni Tavern at the ZCCM-IH Archives in Ndola. Field notes by the author, 6 August 2016.
13. Wisdom Zulu, interview with the author, 18 September 2016, Mpatamatu.
14. See Anonymous (1963). *Buseko* means 'joy', rooted in *-seka*, to laugh.
15. *Kalulu* means 'hare'.
16. Martin Mulenga, second interview with the author, 21 September 2016, Mpatamatu.
17. Field notes by the author, 30 August 2016; Emmanuel Muyutu, interview with the author, 9 September 2016, Mpatamatu.
18. See Spearpoint (1937: 42), Epstein (1958: 4), Powdermaker (1962: 6, 107).
19. For example the 1935 strike in Luanshya; see Russell (1935: 22–29).
20. They had beaten Italy in the 1988 Olympics but died in a plane crash in 1993. See Wilson (2012).
21. Mpatamatu United Football Club secretary, interview with the author, 15 June 2016, Luanshya.
22. Chrispin Mukapile, interview with the author, 26 July 2016, Roan.
23. See ZCCM (1991). Wisdom Zulu, interview with the author, 18 September 2016, Mpatamatu.
24. Resident of Mpatamatu, interview with the author, 4 August 2016, Mpatamatu.
25. At the time of my fieldwork, Hall B housed a carpentry shop, where coffins were made. This was a commodity that everybody ultimately needed at the end of the day, the manager explained to me. John Mwenya, interview with the author, 25 July 2016, Mpatamatu.

26. Samuel Yumba, second interview with the author, 6 August 2016, Mpatamatu.
27. Resident of Luanshya, interview with the author, 8 September 2016, Luanshya.
28. Felix Chanda, interview with the author, 20 July 2016, Baluba.
29. Seed Co is a Zimbabwean agribusiness specializing in hybrid maize seeds and active in southern and eastern Africa; see Seed Co (2018). Field notes by the author, 20 September 2016.
30. See Department of Cultural Services Copperbelt Province (1991); Wisdom Zulu, interview with the author, 18 September 2016, Mpatamatu.
31. MPACE student union representatives, interview with the author, 1 September 2016, Mpatamatu.
32. See Ferguson (1997: 145), Larmer (2004: 222), Frederiksen (2010: 250–51), Mususa (2010: 383).
33. The 'flats' are two-storey apartment blocks, an architectural rarity in the otherwise monotonous sea of category 5A mine houses of Mpatamatu. See RST Roan Antelope Division (1962d: drawing number 518-1628/4).
34. Agness and Steven Mulenga, interview with the author, 7 June 2016, Mpatamatu.
35. Steven Mulenga, site inspection with the author, 20 June 2016, Mpatamatu.
36. Field notes by the author, 24 July 2016.
37. Field notes by the author, 7 August 2016.
38. Anthony Kabwe, first interview with the author, 16 June 2016, Mpatamatu.
39. See Chalwe (2008: 9–15), Pentecostal Assemblies of Canada (2017), Attanasi (2012: 2).
40. Mercy Tembo, interview with the author, 9 September 2016, Mpatamatu.
41. Anthony Kabwe, first interview with the author, 16 June 2016, Mpatamatu.
42. Andrew Kayekesi, first interview with the author, 28 April 2016, Mpatamatu; Serve Zambia Foundation worker, interview with the author, 20 June 2016, Mpatamatu. I have written about the Serve Zambia Foundation elsewhere; see Straube (2021).
43. Field notes by the author, 5 June, 31 July and 11 September 2016.
44. Justin Mukosha, interview with the author, 7 October 2016, Mpatamatu.
45. The simultaneous use of separate rooms in a single building by individual Pentecostal congregations has also been observed elsewhere; see Butticci (2016: 75).
46. Field notes by the author, 25 September 2016.
47. For quotes from the scriptures, I have chosen the version that most closely resembled the spoken word in the services I attended. This was either the Contemporary English Version (CEV) or the New International Version (NIV).
48. Field notes by the author, 24 July 2016.
49. Field notes by the author, 31 July 2016.
50. Field notes by the author, 25 September 2016.
51. Luke 16:19–31. The question of inequality of incomes was a central theme in Haynes' fieldwork in Kitwe; see Haynes (2012).
52. Field notes by the author, 28 August 2016.
53. Fredrick Mpundu, interview with the author, 1 September 2016, Mpatamatu.
54. Field notes by the author, 3 October 2016.
55. Field notes by the author, 5 June 2016.
56. Field notes by the author, 5 June 2016.

Conclusion
Things Reassembled

In his postcolonial classic *Things Fall Apart*, Chinua Achebe (2001) tells the story of Okonkwo in great detail, his narration revealing the dramatic changes of social relations within Igbo society. I too have based my ethnography on relations of agonism and how they changed in respect to the socio-economic position of particular social groups in Mpatamatu. I wanted to carve out the individuality of the township's residents, their different experiential perspectives on the township's former social welfare buildings, and the practices and strategies they pursued in reappropriating bars, clubs, clinics, community centres and sports facilities. What happened to Mpatamatu's social welfare buildings gave me a glimpse of how people were coping with the post-industrial and, more precisely, post-paternalist processes of ruination that had marked the township since the reprivatization of Zambia's copper sector in 1997.

Mpatamatu was started as a corporate mine township by Roan Antelope Copper Mines (RACM) in 1957. Over a period of twenty years, the township extended ultimately to comprise seven sections, with residential houses for more than twenty thousand people. The mine shaped the lives and material living environment of its labour force through its paternalist practices for forty years. In the 1990s, mine operators started to retreat from those forms of the mine's social investment that lay outside the shafts, pits and plants. This corporate abandonment resulted in the internal restructuring of Mpatamatu. The social welfare buildings were separated from the mine and repurposed as parts of the municipal township of Mpatamatu in the city of Luanshya. I have investigated this repurposing through the reappropriation of the buildings from three different angles.

History gave me an understanding of how the area on which RACM started to mine copper in 1928 was transformed into an extractive sphere by corporate colonialism, how Luanshya was established as a company town, how Mpatamatu and its social welfare buildings were administered under the mine's corporate paternalism, and how the reappropriation of the buildings after the mine had left was informed by the township's corporate past.

Relations offered a way of examining how the material environment and the social order of Mpatamatu mutually informed and interacted with each other. Connections were cut and others newly established. These social and socio-material relations revealed the tremendous changes in the socio-economic positions of men vs. women, miners vs. teachers, and miners vs. preachers.

Materiality uncovered aspects of past corporate social control and opportunity. The former social welfare buildings had separated the locations of work, domesticity and leisure, manifesting the mine's capitalist time regime and gendered division of labour. Simultaneously, the buildings were at the core of community maintenance and reproduction. Left as corporate remains in a municipal township, the buildings resembled the cat in Schrödinger's experiment on the state of quantum superposition: the buildings may possess the potency to both ruin and renovate the community around them at the same time. Only practices of reappropriation collapsed this entanglement into one trajectory or the other.

My fieldwork in Mpatamatu focused on people's interactions with material sites and vice-versa that had been products of imperial practices under British colonialism and transnational capitalism. Corporate paternalism penetrated the socio-industrial project that had turned the rural landscape of the Copperbelt into an urban cluster of towns serving the industry. In light of the copper sector's reprivatization, I chose to move beyond what the industry had first established, maintained, and then left behind in Mpatamatu. Hence, in this book I have examined the reciprocal conditioning of material sites and social action through renovation projects in a ruinous post-paternalist landscape.

Relocation

The local specificities of ruination in Mpatamatu unfolded in the multiple relocations that took place after 1997. The privatization of Zambia Consolidated Copper Mines (ZCCM) resulted in a relocation of capital from the mines as integrated sites of work and life to the mines as exclusive sites of mineral extraction. This relocation ended most of the industry's social investment on the Copperbelt. Since the inception of the industry, mining companies had recognized that production and revenues were linked to maintaining a site of social existence for their labour force. This rationale stemmed from the trajectory of the mining sector, which had constructed the Copperbelt's basic infrastructures in the first place and was competing with other mines in central and southern

Africa for labour in the early days of industrial mining. At the time of ZCCM's privatization, the copper industry's prospects were dim. Investors resisted taking over the responsibility for the mines' social investments in order to cut costs. The mines had shaped people's lives over decades by being present in the residential areas. This presence changed into corporate absence as the relocation of capital destroyed the mines as unitary structures of paternalism.

Mpatamatu changed from being the most comprehensively planned mine township in Luanshya on the front line of the mine's production to being an abandoned municipal township in the periphery of Luanshya. Chapter 1 showed the township as a multi-layered place related to the Lamba people, colonial conquest and memorization, capitalist investment, scientific ore extraction, medicalization, segregationist town planning, corporate paternalism, social opportunity and post-paternalist ruination. Most of the mine's former infrastructures outside the mine's production area were reassigned as the responsibility of private businesses, the municipality, the province and the state. It became the government's obligation to provide and maintain the basic infrastructures in order to safeguard 'the operations of the market' (Comaroff and Comaroff 2000: 324). However, private actors and the government could not step in as fast or as comprehensively as the mine had left. Moreover, the mine operators retained their presence in selected areas. This selective presence of corporate social responsibility (CSR) reproduced colonial spatial hierarchies within the city of Luanshya. The corporate facilities still being run by CNMC Luanshya Copper Mines (CLM) in Luanshya were concentrated in the town centre: the recreation club, the mine hospital, the Trust School and the Craft Training School. The company's Director's Lodge, an exclusive walled-in residential compound for Chinese management staff, was located in the former European mine township. The further I moved away from this area downtown towards Roan and Mpatamatu townships, the less discernible was the mine's presence and the more visibly broken were the infrastructures. In Mpatamatu, one dilapidated mine clinic run by CLM represented all that was left of the mine's social investment. Its material and professional condition prevented it from being recognized as a CSR measure by the township's residents.

Economic activity relocated from the mine and its facilities to Mpatamatu's households, the privatized former mine houses. At the time of my fieldwork, a minority of Mpatamatu's residents were employed by CLM or one of its subcontractors. Labour had relocated itself from predominantly male formal wage employment to small-scale trade and agricultural subsistence, previously female domains of economic activity. In Chapter 2, I showed how the gendered division of labour dissolved into a situational assessment of how men and women respectively could best maintain their families' livelihoods. Women's income-generating strategies, adopted to lower their dependence on men and generate a separate income from their husband's wage under corporate paternalism, became the economic basis of their households. Interestingly, the skills that women had acquired at the community centres, corporate facilities that had substantiated the paternalistic, male-dominated order of the mine, turned out to be skills that enabled women to replace the formal employment of men. My research participants cultivated their back gardens and undeveloped land along the streets of Mpatamatu, in the Nkulumashiba *dambo* and adjacent to the township. Making a livelihood meant not only going into 'the bush', but also bringing it into the township. The relocation of economic activity changed the relationship between men and women. It fragmented Mpatamatu's urban character rooted in corporate town planning.

Renovation

I chose to investigate what had been left not from the perspective of the material remains and the forces that had created them, but from the perspective of the relation between the material remains and those who reappropriated them. The creative interaction between the material characteristics of Mpatamatu's abandoned social welfare buildings and people's private reappropriation of them caught my attention. This interaction was related to residents' experience of the township under corporate paternalism and the changing relationships among particular social groups within its population after the decline of corporate paternalism. Private renovation projects countered the process of material and social ruination.

These renovation projects revived Mpatamatu's former social welfare buildings. Former mineworkers, teachers and preachers reused the buildings in new capacities or restored aspects of their previous functions. The examples of the pay line buildings and the community centres in Chapter 3 showed how the buildings' position within Mpatamatu was renewed. Social welfare buildings that had represented the male paternalist order of the mine and female domesticity became private educational facilities creating social opportunities in the township. Renovation brought the buildings back to life.

Renovation also took up the material characteristics of Mpatamatu's former social welfare buildings. Their material durability made reappropriations possible, cutting across ongoing material decay. Their spatial arrangements, as in the case of the community centres, invited very particular renovative practices. Spaces in other buildings were manipulated to house new functions and provide room for new initiatives. Renovation fused materiality with collective social action and individual human agency.

The material renovation of Mpatamatu's former social welfare building was also mirrored by social renovation, a transition I addressed in Chapter 3. The teachers who founded the township's private schools in the former social welfare buildings had belonged to a subaltern class. They had been government employees in a corporate township, both integrated into and separated within the township at the same time. Mineworkers had been privileged in their access to the mine's infrastructures. As new sitting tenants of the former corporate buildings, however, teachers took over the responsibility for the buildings and determined the terms of access. Similarly, the priests and elders of the Pentecostal Assemblies of God (Zambia) (PAOG(Z)) decided who could use the former sports complex. This authority was mirrored in the fact that the student union leaders at the Mpatamatu College of Education (MPACE) were very much aware of it when they organized a concert. Renovation was a socio-material process that restructured both social positions and material access.

Reintegration

The privatization of ZCCM's Luanshya Division separated the mine from the material sites of its corporate provisions in Mpatamatu. Simultaneously it separated the township's residents from material sites that had played a role in their everyday lives. The unitary structure of the mine, which had integrated different infrastructures under the mine's authority, ceased to exist. The abandonment of the social welfare buildings resulted in the abolition of services, subsidies and programmes, that is, of the social opportunities that had been provided to Mpatamatu's residents. I wanted to know how reappropriations of the abandoned social welfare buildings realigned them with the changing living conditions in the post-paternalist township.

The reintegration of the former social welfare buildings into Mpatamatu was related to the buildings' old and new functions. At the time of my fieldwork, most taverns and clubs remained sites of sociality, exchanges of news and public debates. Mine clinics had been taken over by the Ministry of Health and a health-related non-governmental organization (NGO). The community centres had changed from being pillars of the mine's gendered division of labour between the shaft and the home to private schools extending educational opportunities. Teachers' initiatives became a catalyst in a process that made constructive use of the corporate remains. Other buildings, like the Kabulangeti Tavern, were reintegrated by abandoning their past corporate assignment. As Chapters 3 and 4 showed, reintegration was negotiated between past and present ideas of appropriation, between the past and present needs of the township population.

The ability to assemble people was central to the reintegration of Mpatamatu's former social welfare buildings, as Chapter 4 showed in particular. It was illustrated by taverns and clubs continuing to run in terms of their former functions. It also became evident in the pay line buildings and the community centres that enabled people to study and pray together. The stadium remained a site of football competition, but it was also used for large gatherings. The sports com-

Figure 5.1. The remnants of the entrance to Mpatamatu stadium. Photo by the author.

plex became Mpatamatu's largest house of prayer. On election day, many of the former social welfare buildings housed polling stations. Reintegration happened through people's encounters and collective action under one roof.

The reintegration of Mpatamatu's former social welfare buildings usually went along with a positive assessment of the respective building's spatial setting, material characteristics and inscribed memories. The private schools in the former community centres took advantage of the buildings' classroom structure and continued the centres' educational role. At the sports complex, Sunday services were held with physical intensity, with songs and music reminiscent of the sports activities and concerts of the past. However, this positive approach was not always apparent. In the church at the former Kabulangeti Tavern, memories of the building's past use as a place of drinking that involved intimacies between men and women were evaluated negatively and rejected during services. Reintegration was articulated in line with past aspects of the buildings in terms of both positive appraisal and negative rejections.

Reconnection

Finally, I wanted to understand how the converging processes of ruination and renovation were connected to the global. How did they reposition Mpatamatu in global hierarchies of power? Mpatamatu had turned from being a part of Luanshya's mine to an independent satellite of the city. Its residents had experienced the condition of being put aside and assessed as redundant. From the deterioration of the streets connecting Mpatamatu's sections with each other to the road

leading through Roan and past the tailing dams into Luanshya, from the dismantling of the railway extension to the mine to the broken short-cut road from Luanshya via Fisenge to national highway T3, the infrastructural decay suggested a growing separation of Mpatamatu from Luanshya, the region and the world. In contrast to this disconnection, however, which was rooted in infrastructural decay, I observed multiple processes of reconnection at Mpatamatu's former social welfare buildings.

Mpatamatu was reconnected to Luanshya as a municipal part of town. Ward development committees held regular meetings in the township's former social welfare buildings. The story of the section 26 clinic illustrated how Mpatamatu was reconnected to the national health system under Luanshya's District Health Officer. The Ministry of Education also extended its presence in the township by opening a new primary school in section 27. Reconnection introduced and extended the state's presence in order gradually to take over functions previously provided by the mine.

Institutions started in Mpatamatu's former social welfare buildings after corporate abandonment established new connections between the township and the outside world. The Mpatamatu College of Education (MPACE) produced graduates who were posted to schools in all parts of Zambia and also attracted students from there. The Serve Zambia Foundation, which used the former section 21 clinic as its headquarters, became part of a global network of faith-based NGOs. The foundation facilitated an international exchange involving the township's living conditions. Reconnection resulted in people coming to, leaving and knowing about Mpatamatu.

People reconnected to the world through new modes of dependence. The mine's corporate paternalism had provided social opportunities. It had situated Mpatamatu within a global network of copper-producing communities. Pentecostal churches in the township's former sports complex, pay line buildings and community centres succeeded the mine in forming relationships of dependence that reconnected followers with a global Christian community. They provided new room for residents' claims. Pentecostal movements were present in the former social welfare buildings through their branch churches and the televangelists on the TV screens in Mpatamatu homes. Religion offered a new sense of belonging, of social and entrepreneurial opportunity.

This ethnography has demonstrated the gradual dissolution of a planned corporate spatial order through processes of relocation, renovation, reintegration and reconnection. The planned urban character of Mpatamatu has given way to a space marked physically by agricultural subsistence. Notably, the socio-material processes that I witnessed all possessed a reflexive component. This reflexivity, omnipresent through my recurring usage of the prefix 're-' from the mines' reprivatization to Mpatamatu's reconnection, indicated how much materiality, social experience and history were intertwined in Mpatamatu. It showed the tremendous change in people's living conditions when Zambia's copper sector was restructured in 1997. Nostalgia for past infrastructures was the strongest form of this reflexivity. Ruination with its different histories attached to it was the starting point for the projects of renovation countering it at the township's former social welfare buildings. In contrast to the appropriation of industrial ruins elsewhere (cf. Edensor 2005b: 169), in Mpatamatu it was not the corporate remains that violated normative assignations about township life. This violation was experienced in the corporate abandonment of the former mine township and its consequences outside the corporate remains.

In this book I have shown what people did with what they were left with. I have looked at both the corporate debris that was produced in the absence of the mine as its creator and how this debris was turned into something valuable by township residents. A question that remains with me, going beyond this ethnography, is whether and how ruination comes to an end. From the perspective of Mpatamatu, renovation projects managed to counter material and social decline. However, processes of postcolonial ruination were still present in Luanshya in the form of spatial segregation, socio-economic differentiation and infrastructural decay. It is my hope that the receiver of Roan Antelope Mining Corporation of Zambia (RAMCOZ) will acknowledge the creative initiatives covered in this book.

References

Achebe, C. 2001. *Things Fall Apart*. London: Penguin Books.

Agamben, G. 1998. *Homo Sacer: Sovereign Power and Bare Life*. Stanford: Stanford University Press.

Agar, M.H. 1986. *Speaking of Ethnography*. Beverly Hills: Sage Publications.

———. 1996. *The Professional Stranger: An Informal Introduction to Ethnography*. San Diego: Academic Press.

Akyeampong, E., and C. Ambler. 2002. 'Leisure in African History: An Introduction', *The International Journal of African Historical Studies* 35(1): 1–16.

Alexander, D.J. 1983. 'Problems of Educational Reform in Zambia', *International Journal of Educational Development* 3(2): 203–22.

Ambler, C. 1992. 'Alcohol and the Control of Labor on the Copperbelt', in J. Crush and C. Ambler (eds), *Liquor and Labor in Southern Africa*. Athens: Ohio University Press, pp. 339–66.

Ambler, C., and J. Crush. 1992. 'Alcohol in Southern African Labor History', in J. Crush and C. Ambler (eds), *Liquor and Labor in Southern Africa*. Athens: Ohio University Press, pp. 1–55.

Anderson, B. 2006. *Imagined Communities: Reflections on the Origin and Spread of Nationalism*. London: Verso.

Anonymous. 1963. 'Buseko Club: Biographical Sketch from Inception to Date', 11.6.4B. ZCCM-IH Archives, Ndola.

Arndt, C. 2010. 'High Hopes for Zambia's Copperbelt Ghost Town', *Mail & Guardian*, 23 July. Retrieved 24 September 2020 from https://mg.co.za/article/2010-07-23-high-hopes-for-zambias-copperbelt-ghost-town.

Arndt, S., and A. Hornscheidt. 2009. *Afrika und die deutsche Sprache: Ein kritisches Nachschlagewerk*. Münster: UNRAST.

Attanasi, K. 2012. 'Introduction: The Plurality of Prosperity Theologies and Pentecostalisms', in K. Attanasi and A. Yong (eds), *Pentecostalism and Prosperity: The Socio-Economics of the Global Charismatic Movement*. New York: Palgrave Macmillan, pp. 1–12.

Bates, R.H. 1971. *Unions, Parties, and Political Development: A Study of Mineworkers in Zambia*. New Haven: Yale University Press.

Bauman, Z. 2008. *Wasted Lives: Modernity and Its Outcasts*. Cambridge: Polity Press.

Beatty, A.C. 1931a. 'Discovery of the Roan and Rietbok Claims by William Collier, 1930', October, 12.7.4B. ZCCM-IH Archives, Ndola.

———. 1931b. 'High Lights of Rhodesian Copper Mining', *Mining and Metallurgy* 12: 518–21.

Benjamin, W. 2002. *The Arcades Project*, trans. H. Eiland and K. McLaughlin. Cambridge: Harvard University Press.

Bigon, L. 2013. 'Garden Cities in Colonial Africa: A Note on Historiography', *Planning Perspectives* 28(3): 477–85.

Boym, S. 2001. *The Future of Nostalgia*. New York: Basic Books.

———. 2011. 'Ruinophilia: Appreciation of Ruins', *Atlas of Transformation*. Retrieved 24 September 2020 from http://monumenttotransformation.org/atlas-of-transformation/html/r/ruinophilia/ruinophilia-appreciation-of-ruins-svetlana-boym.html.

Bradley, K. 1952. *Copper Venture: The Discovery and Development of Roan Antelope and Mufulira*. London: Parrish.

Branigan, P.F. 1956. *Commission Appointed to Inquire into the Unrest in the Mining Industry in Northern Rhodesia in Recent Months*. Lusaka: Government Printer.

Branson, N. 2016. 'Zambia: Expert Briefing', Africa Research Institute. Retrieved 10 February 2017 from http://www.africaresearchinstitute.org/zambia-expert-briefing/.

Brown, R. 1966. *Report of the Commission of Inquiry into the Mining Industry*. Lusaka: Government Printer.

Bruce, B. 2012. '110 Years – And Built To Last', *Robust* (March).

Buell, R.L. 1928. *The Native Problem in Africa*. New York: The Macmillan Company.

Burawoy, M. 1972a. *The Colour of Class on the Copper Mines: From African Advancement to Zambianization*. Manchester: Manchester University Press.

———. 1972b. 'Another Look at the Mineworker', *African Social Research* 14: 239–87.

———. 1998. 'The Extended Case Method', *Sociological Theory* 16(1): 4–33.

————. 2013. 'Ethnographic Fallacies: Reflections on Labour Studies in the Era of Market Fundamentalism', *Work, Employment and Society* 27(3): 526–36.

Butler, L.J. 2007. *Copper Empire: Mining and the Colonial State in Northern Rhodesia, c. 1930–1964*. New York: Palgrave Macmillan.

Butticci, A. 2016. *African Pentecostals in Catholic Europe: Politics of Presence in the Twenty-First Century*. Cambridge: Harvard University Press.

Cane, J. 2019. *Civilising Grass: The Art of the Lawn on the South African Highveld*. Johannesburg: Wits University Press.

Casey, E.S. 1987. 'The World of Nostalgia', *Man and World* 20: 361–84.

Casid, J.H. 2011. 'Epilogue: Landscape In, Around, and Under the Performative', *Women and Performance* 21(1): 97–116.

Certeau, M. de. 1988. *The Practice of Everyday Life*, trans. S. Rendall. Berkeley: University of California Press.

Chalwe, A. 2008. 'An Evaluation of the Mission History of Pentecostal Assemblies of God in Zambia', Ph.D. dissertation. Potchefstroom: North-West University.

Charter Consolidated Limited International Appointments Division. 1970. 'An Opportunity in Zambia', *The Observer*, 23 August.

Chansa, J.C. 2020. 'State, Mining Companies and Communities: A History of Environmental Pollution in Zambia (1964 to the Present)', Ph.D. dissertation. Bloemfontein: University of the Free State.

Chauncey, G.J. 1981. 'The Locus of Reproduction: Women's Labour in the Zambian Copperbelt, 1927–1953', *Journal of Southern African Studies* 7(2): 135–64.

Chileshe, A. 2017. 'Lungu Takes a Drive through Roan', *The Mast Online*, 16 October. Retrieved 24 September 2020 from https://www.themastonline .com/2017/10/16/lungu-takes-a-drive-%E2%80%A8through-roan%E2% 80%A8-%E2%80%A8/.

Chipande, H.D. 2016. 'Mining for Goals: Football and Social Change on the Zambian Copperbelt, 1940s–1960s', *Radical History Review* 125: 55–73.

Cleveland, T. 2015. *Diamonds in the Rough: Corporate Paternalism on the Mines of Colonial Angola, 1917–1975*. Athens: Ohio University Press.

Clifford, J. 1997. 'Spatial Practices: Fieldwork, Travel, and the Disciplining of Anthropology', in A. Gupta and J. Ferguson (eds), *Anthropological Locations: Boundaries and Grounds of a Field Science*. Berkeley: University of California Press, pp. 185–222.

Clifford Chance. 1997. 'Development Agreement: The Government of the Republic of Zambia and Roan Antelope Mining Corporation of Zambia plc', 14 October, document courtesy of RAID, London.

CNMC. 2011. 'Organizational Structure'. Retrieved 24 September 2020 from http://www.cnmc.com.cn/outlineen.jsp?column_no=1204.

Coetzee, A.J.P. 1953. 'Malaria Control at Nkana Mine', in M. Watson (ed.), *African Highway: The Battle for Health in Central Africa*. London: John Murray, pp. 148–50.

Cohen, P.A. 2003. 'Reflections on a Watershed Date: The 1949 Divide in Chinese History', in J.N. Wasserstrom (ed.), *Twentieth-Century China: New Approaches*. London: Routledge, pp. 27–36.

Coleman, F.L. 1971. *The Northern Rhodesian Copperbelt 1899–1962*. Manchester: Manchester University Press.

Collier, S.J. 2009. 'Topologies of Power: Foucault's Analysis of Political Government beyond "Governmentality"', *Theory, Culture & Society* 26(6): 78–108.

Collings & Schaerer Town Planning Consultants Consulting Engineers. 1962. 'Mpatamatu Sports Centre and Western School Site in Precinct No. 4', 30 July, 10.6.10D. ZCCM-IH Archives, Ndola.

Comaroff, J., and J.L. Comaroff. 2000. 'Millenial Capitalism: First Thoughts on a Second Coming', *Public Culture* 12(2): 291–343.

Confucius Institute at the University of Zambia. 2018. 'Luanshya Trust School', University of Zambia. Retrieved 17 August 2018 from https://www.unza .zm/confucius/luanshya-trust-school.

Copperbelt Basic and Secondary Schools Heads' Association. 1992. 'Invitation to 1992 Colgate Sponsored Inter-Provincial Athletics Championship for Secondary Schools', 11 August, 3.4.4E. ZCCM-IH Archives, Ndola.

Costain Group. 2015. 'Our History'. Retrieved 24 September 2020 from https:// www.costain.com/about-us/our-history/.

Craig, J. 1999. 'State Enterprise and Privatisation in Zambia 1968–1998: State Enterprise and Privatisation', Ph.D. dissertation. Leeds: University of Leeds.

———. 2001. 'Putting Privatisation into Practice: The Case of Zambia Consolidated Copper Mines Limited', *Journal of Modern African Studies* 39(3): 389–410.

Crang, M. 2011. 'Michel de Certeau', in P. Hubbard and R. Kitchin (eds), *Key Thinkers on Space and Place*. London: Sage, pp. 106–12.

Crawford, M. 1995. *Building the Workingman's Paradise: The Design of American Company Towns*. London: Verso.

Cross, J.S.W. 1973. 'The Watch Tower Movement in South Central Africa 1908–1945', Ph.D. dissertation. Oxford: Oxford University.

Cunningham, S. 1981. *The Copper Industry in Zambia: Foreign Mining Companies in a Developing Country*. New York: Praeger Publishers.

Dalzell, A.C. 1953a. 'Report of Anti-Malarial Work during the Year 1931', in M. Watson (ed.), *African Highway: The Battle for Health in Central Africa*. London: John Murray, pp. 47–53.

———. 1953b. 'Report of Anti-Malarial Work during the Year 1932', in M. Watson (ed.), *African Highway: The Battle for Health in Central Africa*. London: John Murray, pp. 54–58.

Davies, C. 1989. 'Goffman's Concept of the Total Institution: Criticisms and Revisions', *Human Studies* 12: 77–95.

Davis, J.M. 1967. *Modern Industry and the African*. New York: Augustus M. Kelley.

Dawdy, S.L. 2010. 'Clockpunk Anthropology and the Ruins of Modernity', *Current Anthropology* 51(6): 761–93.

Demissie, F. 1998. 'In the Shadow of the Gold Mines: Migrancy and Mine Housing in South Africa', *Housing Studies* 13(4): 445–69.

Department of Cultural Services Copperbelt Province. 1991. 'Music Competition Main Programme', 21 December, 3.4.4E. ZCCM-IH Archives, Ndola.

Desjarlais, R. 2003. *Sensory Biographies: Lives and Deaths among Nepal's Yolmo Buddhists*. Berkeley: University of California Press.

Devisch, R. 1996. '"Pillaging Jesus": Healing Churches and the Villagisation of Kinshasa', *Africa: Journal of the International African Institute* 66(4): 555–86.

———. 1998. 'Colonial State Building in the Congo, and Its Dismantling', *Journal of Legal Pluralism and Unofficial Law* 30(42): 221–44.

Dolan, C. and D. Rajak. 2016. 'Introduction: Toward the Anthropology of Corporate Social Responsibility', in C. Dolan and D. Rajak (eds), *The Anthropology of Corporate Social Responsibility*. New York: Berghahn Books, pp. 1–28.

Donge, J.K.v. 2009. 'The Plundering of Zambian Resources by Frederick Chiluba and His Friends: A Case Study of the Interaction between National Politics and the International Drive Towards Good Governance', *African Affairs* 108(430): 69–90.

Dow. 2018. 'Über den ValuePark'. Retrieved 22 August 2018 from https://de.dow.com/de-de/standorte/mitteldeutschland/valuepark/uber-den-valuepark.

Eccles, L.W.G. 1946. *Northern Rhodesia: Report of the Land Commission*. Lusaka: Government Printer.

ECZ. 2016. '2016 Zambia Elections Results: ECZ Verified Results', *The Zambian Observer*, 13 August. Retrieved 7 February 2018 from http://www.zambianobserver.com/2016-zambia-elections-results-ecz-verified-results/.

Edensor, T. 2005a. 'The Ghosts of Industrial Ruins: Ordering and Disordering Memory in Excessive Space', *Environment and Planning D: Society and Space* 23(6): 829–49.

———. 2005b. *Industrial Ruins: Space, Aesthetics and Materiality*. New York: Berg.

Englund, H. 2002. 'The Village in the City, the City in the Village: Migrants in Lilongwe', *Journal of Southern African Studies* 28(1): 137–54.

Epstein, A.L. 1958. *Politics in an Urban African Community*. Manchester: Manchester University Press.

———. 1992. *Scenes from African Urban Life: Collected Copperbelt Papers*. Edinburgh: Edinburgh University Press.

Evans, A. 2015. 'History Lessons for Gender Equality from the Zambian Copperbelt, 1900–1990', *Gender, Place & Culture* 22(3): 344–62.

Faber, M. 1971a. 'The Mshiri-Thomson Meeting in November 1890: A Note', *African Social Research* 12: 129–43.

———. 1971b. 'Corporate Policy on the Copperbelt', in M.L.O. Faber and J.G. Potter (eds), *Towards Economic Independence: Papers on the Nationalisation of the Copper Industry in Zambia*. London: Cambridge University Press, pp. 14–39.

Federation of Rhodesia and Nyasaland Ministry of Health–Northern Rhodesia. 1959. 'African Welfare Clinic: Mpatamatu Clinic R.A.C.M. LTD.: Report for the Month of December 1959', December, 12.7.3B. ZCCM-IH Archives, Ndola.

Ferguson, J. 1990a. 'Mobile Workers, Modernist Narratives: A Critique of the Historiography of Transition on the Zambian Copperbelt [Part One]', *Journal of Southern African Studies* 16(3): 385–412.

———. 1990b. 'Mobile Workers, Modernist Narratives: A Critique of the Historiography of Transition on the Zambian Copperbelt [Part Two]', *Journal of Southern African Studies* 16(4): 603–21.

———. 1994. 'Modernist Narratives, Conventional Wisdoms, and Colonial Liberalism: Reply to a Straw Man', *Journal of Southern African Studies* 20(4): 633–40.

———. 1997. 'The Country and the City on the Copperbelt', in A. Gupta and J. Ferguson (eds), *Culture, Power, Place: Explorations in Critical Anthropology*. Durham: Duke University Press, pp. 137–54.

———. 1999. *Expectations of Modernity: Myths and Meanings of Urban Life on the Zambian Copperbelt*. Berkeley: University of California Press.

———. 2006. *Global Shadows: Africa in the Neoliberal World Order*. Durham: Duke University Press.

———. 2009. 'Global Disconnect: Abjection and the Aftermath of Modernism', in M. Mollona, G. De Neve and J. Parry (eds), *Industrial Work and Life: An Anthropological Reader*. Oxford: Berg, pp. 311–29.

———. 2013. 'Declarations of Dependence: Labour, Personhood, and Welfare in Southern Africa', *Journal of the Royal Anthropological Institute* 19: 223–42.

Finn, J.L. 1998. *Tracing the Veins: Of Copper, Culture, and Community from Butte to Chuquicamata*. Berkeley: University of California Press.

Forster, J. 1940. *Report of the Commission Appointed to Inquire into the Disturbances in the Copperbelt, Northern Rhodesia*. Lusaka: Government Printer.

Foucault, M. 1982. 'The Subject and Power', *Critical Inquiry* 8(4): 777–95.

———. 1995. *Discipline and Punishment: The Birth of the Prison*, trans. A. Sheridan. New York: Vintage Books.

———. 1998. *The Will to Knowledge*, trans. R. Hurley. London: Penguin Books.

Fraser, A. 2010. 'Introduction: Boom and Bust on the Zambian Copperbelt', in A. Fraser and M. Larmer (eds), *Zambia, Mining, and Neoliberalism: Boom and Bust on the Globalized Copperbelt*. New York: Palgrave Macmillan, pp. 1–30.

Fraser, A., and J. Lungu. 2007. *For Whom the Windfalls? Winners and Losers in the Privatisation of Zambia's Copper Mines*. Lusaka: Civil Society Network of Zambia.

Frederiksen, T. 2010. 'Unearthing Rule: Mining, Power and the Political Ecology of Extraction in Colonial Zambia', Ph.D. dissertation. Manchester: University of Manchester.

———. 2013. 'Seeing the Copperbelt: Science, Mining and Colonial Power in Northern Rhodesia', *Geoforum* 44: 271–81.

———. 2014. 'Authorizing the "Natives": Governmentality, Dispossession, and the Contradictions of Rule in Colonial Zambia', *Annals of the Association of American Geographers* 104(6): 1273–90.

Gann, L.H. 1964. *A History of Northern Rhodesia: Early Days to 1953*. London: Chatto & Windus.

Gardiner, J. 1970. 'Some Aspects of the Establishment of Towns in Zambia during the Nineteen Twenties and Thirties', *Zambian Urban Studies* 3: 1–33.

Geertz, C. 2006. *The Interpretation of Cultures: Selected Essays*. New York: Basic Books.

Gewald, J.-B., and S. Soeters. 2010. 'African Miners and Shape-Shifting Capital Flight: The Case of Luanshya/Baluba', in A. Fraser and M. Larmer (eds), *Zambia, Mining, and Neoliberalism: Boom and Bust on the Globalized Copperbelt*. New York: Palgrave Macmillan, pp. 155–83.

Gluckman, M. 1940. 'Analysis of a Social Situation in Modern Zululand', *Bantu Studies* 14(1): 1–30.

———. 1956. 'Social Anthropology in Central Africa', *Rhodes-Livingstone Journal* 20: 1–27.

———. 2006. 'Ethnographic Data in British Social Anthropology', in T.M.S. Evens and D. Handelman (eds), *The Manchester School: Practice and Ethnographic Praxis in Anthropology*. New York: Berghahn Books, pp. 13–22.

Göbel, H.K. 2015. *The Re-Use of Urban Ruins: Atmospheric Inquiries of the City*. New York: Routledge.

Godoy, R. 1985. 'Mining: Anthropological Perspectives', *Annual Review of Anthropology* 14: 199–217.

Goffman, E. 1990. *Asylums: Essays on the Social Situation of Mental Patients and Other Inmates*. New York: Anchor Books.

Gordillo, G.R. 2014. *Rubble: The Afterlife of Destruction*. Durham: Duke University Press.

Gordon, R.J. 1977. *Mines, Masters and Migrants: Life in a Namibian Mine Compound*. Johannesburg: Ravan Press.

Grant Thornton. 2004. 'RAMCOZ (in receivership) Properties To Be Advertised for Sale', 26 February, Office of the Receiver, Luanshya.

Guo Chatelard, S. 2011. 'Unpacking the New "Scramble for Africa": A Critical and Local Perspective of Chinese Activities in Zambia', in J.L. de Sales Marques, R. Seidelmann and A. Vasilache (eds), *States, Regions and the Global System: Europe and Northern Asia-Pacific in Globalised Governance*. Baden-Baden: Nomos, pp. 175–99.

Gupta, A. 2015. 'Suspension', *Cultural Anthropology*, 24 September. Retrieved 1 March 2018 from https://culanth.org/fieldsights/suspension.

Gupta, P. 2015. 'Decolonization and (Dis)Possession in Lusophone Africa', in D. Vigneswaran and J. Quirk (eds), *Mobility Makes States: Migration and Power in Africa*. Philadelphia: University of Pennsylvania Press, pp. 169–93.

———. 2019. *Portuguese Decolonization in the Indian Ocean World: History and Ethnography*. London: Bloomsbury Academic.

Hailey, W.M. 1950. *Native Administration in the British African Territories: Part II, Central Africa: Zanzibar, Nyasaland, Northern Rhodesia*. London: His Majesty's Stationery Office.

Hain, S., and S. Stroux. 1996. *Die Salons der Sozialisten: Kulturhäuser der DDR*. Berlin: Ch. Links Verlag.

Handelman, D. 2006. 'The Extended Case: Interactional Foundations and Prospective Dimensions', in T.M.S. Evens and D. Handelman (eds), *The Manchester School: Practice and Ethnographic Praxis in Anthropology*. New York: Berghahn Books, pp. 94–117.

Harper, R. 1966. *Nostalgia: An Existential Exploration of Longing and Fulfilment in the Modern Age*. Cleveland: Press of Western Reserve University.

Harries-Jones, P. 1964. 'Marital Disputes and the Process of Concilliation in a Copperbelt Town', *Rhodes-Livingstone Journal* 25: 29–72.

———. 1975. *Freedom and Labour: Mobilization and Political Control on the Zambian Copperbelt*. Oxford: Basil Blackwell.

Hartnack, A.M.C. 2016. *Ordered Estates: Welfare, Power and Maternalism on Zimbabwe's (Once White) Highveld*. Harare: Weaver Press.

Hartung, U. 1997. *Arbeiter- und Bauerntempel: DDR-Kulturhäuser der fünfziger Jahre*. Berlin: Schelzky & Jeep.

Haynes, N. 2012. 'Pentecostalism and the Morality of Money: Prosperity, Inequality, and Religious Sociality on the Zambian Copperbelt', *Journal of the Royal Anthropological Institute* 18: 123–39.

———. 2017. *Moving by the Spirit: Pentecostal Social Life on the Zambian Copperbelt*. Oakland: University of California Press.

Higginson, J. 1989. *A Working Class in the Making: Belgian Colonial Labor Policy, Private Enterprise, and the African Mineworker, 1907–1951*. Madison: University of Wisconsin Press.

Hobson, D. 1961. 'Chirupula Stephenson: The Man and the Myth', *Horizon* (May): 20–24.

Home, R. 1997. *Of Planting and Planning: The Making of British Colonial Cities.* London: E & FN Spon.

———. 2000. 'From Barrack Compounds to the Single-Family House: Planning Worker Housing in Colonial Natal and Northern Rhodesia', *Planning Perspectives* 15: 327–47.

———. 2013. 'Introduction', in R. Home (ed.), *Lusaka: The New Capital of Northern Rhodesia.* Abingdon: Routledge, pp. 1–25.

———. 2015. 'Colonial Urban Planning in Anglophone Africa', in C.N. Silva (ed.), *Urban Planning in Sub-Saharan Africa: Colonial and Post-Colonial Planning Cultures.* New York: Routledge, pp. 53–66.

Horizon. 1959a. 'Factors Which Have Affected the Copper Price since 1900' (February): 21.

———. 1959b. 'A Place in the Sun for the African Mineworker' (June): 4–8.

———. 1960. 'Cecil Spearpoint Retires' (March): 41.

———. 1963. 'Boniface Kaloko, Welfare Officer, Roan Antelope' (April): 18–20.

———. 1964. 'Aerial Photograph of Section 23' (April): back cover.

———. 1965. 'Part II of RST's Story: War Starts a New Copperbelt Era' (January): 20–25.

———. 1968. 'Training Scheme for Luanshya's Youth' (January): 28–33.

———. 1970a. 'Progress is Contrast' (April): 10–17.

———. 1970b. 'Rosa Pensulo Kunda' (February): 3.

Howe, C., et al. 2016. 'Paradoxical Infrastructures: Ruins, Retrofit, and Risk', *Science, Technology, & Human Values* 41(3): 547–65.

Hughes, E.C. 2010. 'Memorandum on Total Institutions', *Sociologica* 2: 1–7.

Jønsson, J.B., and D.F. Bryceson. 2014. 'Going for Gold: Miners' Mobility and Mining Motivation', in D.F. Bryceson, E. Fisher, J.B. Jønsson and R. Mwaipopo (eds), *Mining and Social Transformation in Africa: Mineralizing and Democratizing Trends in Artisanal Production.* London: Routledge, pp. 25–43.

Kalu, O. 2008. *African Pentecostalism: An Introduction.* Oxford: Oxford University Press.

Kambwili, C. 2008. 'Remarks by Member of Parliament Chishimba Kambwili during the Daily Parliamentary Debates for the Second Session of the Tenth Assembly', 13 August. Retrieved 24 September 2020 from http://www.parliament.gov.zm/node/1730.

Kanduza, A.M. 1981. 'Teachers' Strike, 1970: A Chapter in Zambia's Labour History', *Histoire Sociale – Social History* 14(28): 485–507.

Kapferer, B. 2006. 'Situations, Crisis, and the Anthropology of the Concrete: The Contribution of Max Gluckman', in T.M.S. Evens and D. Handelman (eds), *The Manchester School: Practice and Ethnographic Praxis in Anthropology.* New York: Berghahn Books, pp. 118–55.

Katasefa, Z. 2009. 'LCM Announces Complete Pullout', *The Post*, 17 January. Retrieved 22 August 2018 from http://maravi.blogspot.com/2009/01/lcm-announces-complete-pullout.html.

Kaunda, F. 2002. *Selling the Family Silver: The Zambian Copper Mines Story.* Lusaka: F. Kaunda.

Kaunda, J. 1999. 'Zambia: Luanshya Risks Turning into a Ghost Town', *The Post*, 4 November.

Kaunda, K., and C. Morris. 1960. *Black Government? A Discussion between Colin Morris and Kenneth Kaunda.* Lusaka: United Society for Christian Literature.

Kazimbaya-Senkwe, B. Mwila and S.C. Guy. 2007. 'Back to the Future? Privatisation and the Domestication of Water in the Copperbelt Province of Zambia, 1900–2000', *Geoforum* 38: 869–85.

King, A.D. 1980. 'Exporting Planning: The Colonial and Neo-colonial Experience', in G.E. Cherry (ed.), *Shaping an Urban World.* New York: St. Martin's Press, pp. 203–26.

Kline, A.S. 2004. 'Ovid: Fasti Book Four', *Poetry in Translation.* Retrieved 1 February 2018 from http://www.poetryintranslation.com/PITBR/Latin/Ovid FastiBkFour.php#anchor_Toc69367852.

Knight, J.B. 1971. 'Wages and Zambia's Economic Development', in C. Elliott (ed.), *Constraints on the Economic Development of Zambia.* London: Oxford University Press, pp. 91–119.

Kopytoff, I. 2011. 'The Cultural Biography of Things: Commoditization as Process', in A. Appadurai (ed.), *The Social Life of Things: Commodities in Cultural Perspective.* Cambridge: Cambridge University Press, pp. 64–91.

Krishnamurthy, B.S. 1969. 'The Thomson Treaties and the Johnston's Certificate of Claim', *African Social Research* 8: 588–601.

Lankton, L. 1991. *Cradle to Grave: Life, Work, and Death at the Lake Superior Copper Mines.* Oxford: Oxford University Press.

Larkin, B. 2008. *Signal and Noise: Media, Infrastructure, and Urban Culture in Nigeria.* Durham: Duke University Press.

Larmer, M. 2004. '"If We Are Still Here Next Year": Zambian Historical Research in the Context of Decline, 2002–2003', *History in Africa* 31: 215–29.

———. 2005. 'Reaction and Resistance to Neo-liberalism in Zambia', *Review of African Political Economy* 32(103): 29–45.

———. 2007. *Mineworkers in Zambia: Labour and Political Change in Post-Colonial Africa.* London: Tauris Academic Studies.

Larmer, M., and A. Fraser. 2007. 'Of Cabbages and King Cobra: Populist Politics and Zambia's 2006 Election', *African Affairs* 106(425): 611–37.

Larmer, M., and V. Laterza. 2017. 'Contested Wealth: Social and Political Mobilisation in Extractive Communities in Africa', *The Extractive Industries and Society* 4(4): 701–6.

Laterza, V., and P. Mususa. 2015. 'Zambia's Uncertain Future: Political Rifts and Economic Challenges in Lusaka', *Foreign Affairs*, 4 March. Retrieved 10 February 2017 from https://www.foreignaffairs.com/articles/africa/2015-03-04/zambias-uncertain-future.

Law, K. 2011. '"Even a Labourer Is Worthy of His Hire: How Much More a Wife?" Gender and the Contested Nature of Domesticity in Colonial Zimbabwe, c. 1945–1978', *South African Historical Journal* 63(3): 456–74.

LeBas, A. 2007. 'The Politics of Institutional Subversion: Organized Labour and Resistance in Zambia', in J. Chalcraft and Y. Noorani (eds), *Counterhegemony in the Colony and Postcolony*. New York: Palgrave Macmillan, pp. 228–51.

Lee, C.K. 2009. 'Raw Encounters: Chinese Managers, African Workers and the Politics of Casualization in Africa's Chinese Enclaves', *The China Quarterly* 199: 647–66.

Letcher, O. 1932. *South Central Africa: An Outline of the History, Geography, Commerce and Transportation Systems of the Congo-Zambezi Watershed, with Special Reference to the Mineral Industry*. Johannesburg: African Publications.

Leubuscher, C. 1931. *Der südafrikanische Eingeborene als Industriearbeiter und Stadtbewohner*. Jena: Gustav Fischer.

Lévi-Strauss, C. 1966. *The Savage Mind*. London: Weidenfeld and Nicolson.

Lloyd, M. 1960. '"It's My Job": Mavis Lloyd, African Women's Welfare Officer, Roan Antelope', *Horizon* (April): 27–29.

LMC. 1991. 'Supplementary Valuation Roll 1991: Mpatamatu Township Commercial/Recreational/Others', Office of the Receiver, Luanshya.

Luchembe, C.C. 1982. 'Finance Capital and Mine Labor: A Comparative Study of Copperminers in Zambia and Peru, 1870–1980', Ph.D. dissertation. Los Angeles: University of California.

Lusaka Times. 2008. 'Court Jails Former ZCCM Boss Francis Kaunda', 15 August. Retrieved 1 March 2018 from https://www.lusakatimes.com/2008/08/15/court-jails-former-zccm-boss-francis-kaunda/.

———. 2016. 'Riots Breaks Out in Luanshya after HH and GBM Are Arrested', 5 October. Retrieved 22 August 2018 from https://www.lusakatimes.com/2016/10/05/riots-breaks-luanshya-hh-gbm-arrested/.

———. 2017. 'Reopening of the Baluba Mine to Create Jobs for the Youths – Luanshya Mayor', 5 August. Retrieved 15 February 2018 from https://www.lusakatimes.com/2017/08/05/reopening-baluba-mine-create-jobs-youths-luanshya-mayor/.

Luthar, B., and M. Pušnik. 2010. 'Introduction: The Lure of Utopia, Socialist Everyday Spaces', in B. Luthar and M. Pušnik (eds), *Remembering Utopia: The Culture of Everyday Life in Socialist Yugoslavia*. Washington: New Academia Publishing, pp. 1–33.

Macmillan, H. 1993. 'The Historiography of Transition on the Zambian Copperbelt: Another View', *Journal of Southern African Studies* 19(4): 681–712.

————. 1996. 'More Thoughts on the Historiography of Transition on the Zambian Copperbelt', *Journal of Southern African Studies* 22(2): 309–12.

————. 2012. 'Mining, Housing and Welfare in South Africa and Zambia: A Historical View', *Journal of Contemporary African Studies* 30(4): 539–50.

Mah, A.A. 2008. 'Landscapes and Legacies of Industrial Ruination', Ph.D. dissertation. London: London School of Economics and Political Science.

Mail Reporter. 1966. 'Extract from the *Zambia Mail*', 11.6.4B. ZCCM-IH Archives, Ndola.

Manchishi, X. 2013. 'RAMCOZ Sitting Tenants Appeal to Sata', *Times of Zambia*, January.

Masimba Group. 2013. 'Our History'. Retrieved 27 August 2018 from http://www.masimbagroup.com/index.php/about-us/history.

Massey, D. 2012. *For Space*. Los Angeles: Sage.

McClintock, A. 1995. *Imperial Leather: Race, Gender and Sexuality in the Colonial Contest*. New York: Routledge.

Meebelo, H.S. 1986. *African Proletarians and Colonial Capitalism: The Origins, Growth and Struggles of the Zambian Labour Movement to 1964*. Lusaka: Kenneth Kaunda Foundation.

Mijere, N.N.J. 1985. 'The Mineworkers' Resistance to Governmental Decentralization in Zambia: Nation-Building and Labour Aristocracy in the Third World', Ph.D. dissertation. Waltham: Brandeis University.

Milner-Thornton, J.B. 2012. *The Long Shadow of the British Empire: The Ongoing Legacies of Race and Class in Zambia*. New York: Palgrave Macmillan.

Mitchell, J.C. 1951. 'A Note on the Urbanization of Africans on the Copperbelt', *Rhodes-Livingstone Journal* 12: 20–27.

————. 1954. 'African Urbanization in Ndola and Luanshya', *Rhodes-Livingstone Communication* 6.

Mitchell, W.J.T. 2002. 'Introduction', in W.J.T. Mitchell (ed.), *Landscape and Power*. Chicago: University of Chicagp Press, pp. 1–4.

MMTMB. 1961. 'Memorandum: Mpatamatu Street and Precinct Names', 3 August, T21.2A. ZCCM-IH Archives, Ndola.

————. 1962. 'Minutes of the Twenty-first Meeting of the MMTMB', 29 August, 10.6.10D. ZCCM-IH Archives, Ndola.

————. 1965. 'Board Estimates: 1965 Beer Hall Replacement', 19 January, 16.3.7A. ZCCM-IH Archives, Ndola.

MOFCOM. 2015. 'Untitled', 5 May. Retrieved 23 February 2016 from http://images.mofcom.gov.cn/zm/201505/20150505212927576.xls.

Moodie, T.D. 1994. *Going for Gold: Men, Mines, and Migration*. Berkeley: University of California Press.

Moore, R.J.B. 1948. *These African Copper Miners: A Study of the Industrial Revolution in Northern Rhodesia, with Principal Reference to the Copper Mining Industry*. London: Livingstone Press.

Mugala, F. 2016. 'Life History: Fackson Mugala Proprietor for Suzika Private School', 4 October, personal file to author, Luanshya.

Mukuwa, G. 1981. 'Ndola Rural Villager Seeks to Alter History. . . : "Collier Didn't Shoot that Antelope"', *Mining Mirror*, 28 August.

Mulenga, A. Undated. 'History of Nkulumashiba Secondary School (1983–2015)', Document Courtesy of School's Head Teacher, Mpatamatu.

Mulenga Associates, S.P. 1986a. 'Report and Valuation of Section 23 Tarven', 6 February, 3.4.4G. ZCCM-IH Archives, Ndola.

———. 1986b. 'Report and Valuation on Buseko Club Luanshya', 30 January, 3.4.4G. ZCCM-IH Archives, Ndola.

Mulenga, B. 2017. 'What Zambia Lost: The Mines Social Welfare Infrastructure', *Zambian Eye*, 29 March. Retrieved 26 January 2018 from http://zambianeye.com/what-zambia-lost-the-mines-social-welfare-infrastructure/.

Musonda, C. 2014. 'RAMCOZ Ex-Workers Petition Scott over Social Assets', *Zambia Daily Mail*, 26 November. Retrieved 23 August 2018 from https://www.daily-mail.co.zm/ramcoz-ex-workers-petition-scott-social-assets/.

Musonda, J. 2020. 'Undermining Gender: Women Mineworkers at the Rock Face in a Zambian Underground Mine', *Anthropology Southern Africa* 43(1): 32–42.

Mususa, P. 2010. '"Getting By": Life on the Copperbelt after the Privatisation of Zambia Consolidated Copper Mines', *Social Dynamics* 36(2): 380–94.

———. 2014. 'There Used To Be Order: Life on the Copperbelt after the Privatisation of the Zambia Consolidated Copper Mines', Ph.D. dissertation. Cape Town: University of Cape Town.

Mutale, E. 2004. *The Management of Urban Development in Zambia*. Aldershot: Ashgate.

Mwanakatwe, J.M. 1968. *The Growth of Education in Zambia since Independence*. Lusaka: Oxford University Press.

Myhre, K.C. 2016. 'Introduction', in K.C. Myhre (ed.), *Cutting and Connecting: 'Afrinesian' Perspectives on Networks, Relationality, and Exchange*. New York: Berghahn Books, pp. 1–24.

National Council for Construction. 2015. 'REGISTRATIONS AS AT END OF DAY 25TH JUNE, 2015'. Retrieved 22 February 2016 from http://www.ncc.org.zm/wp-content/uploads/2012/11/REGISTRATIONS-AS-AT-25TH-JUNE-2015.xlsx.

Njoh, A.J. 2009. 'Urban Planning as a Tool of Power and Socio-Political Control in Colonial Africa', *Planning Perspectives* 24(3): 301–17.

Northern Rhodesia. 1964. *White Paper on British South Africa Company's Claims to Mineral Royalties*. Lusaka: Government Printer.

Onselen, C.v. 1976. *Chibaro: African Mine Labour in Southern Rhodesia 1900–1933*. London: Pluto Press.

OpenStreetMap. 2016. 'Node: Mpatamatu'. Retrieved 1 February 2018 from http://www.openstreetmap.org/node/2567143540.

Parpart, J.L. 1983. *Labor and Capital on the African Copperbelt*. Philadelphia: Temple University Press.

———. 1986a. 'Class and Gender on the Copperbelt: Women in Northern Rhodesian Copper Mining Communities, 1926–1964', in C. Robertson and I. Berger (eds), *Women and Class in Africa*. New York: Holmes & Meier Publishers, pp. 141–60.

———. 1986b. 'The Household and the Mine Shaft: Gender and Class Struggle on the Zambian Copperbelt, 1926–64', *Journal of Southern African Studies* 13(1): 36–56.

Parry, J.P. 1999. 'Lords of Labour: Working and Shirking in Bhilai', in J.P. Parry, J. Breman and K. Kapadia (eds), *The Worlds of Indian Industrial Labour*. London: Sage Publications, pp. 107–40.

Pentecostal Assemblies of Canada. 2017. 'About'. Retrieved 12 October 2017 from https://paoc.org/family/story.

Perrings, C. 1979. *Black Mineworkers in Central Africa*. London: Heinemann.

Peša, I. 2017. 'Sawdust Pellets, Micro Gasifying Cook Stoves and Charcoal in Urban Zambia: Understanding the Value Chain Dynamics of Improved Cook Stove Initiatives', *Sustainable Energy Technologies and Assessments* 22: 171–76.

———. 2020. 'Crops and Copper: Agriculture and Urbanism on the Central African Copperbelt, 1950–2000', *Journal of Southern African Studies* 46(3): 527–45.

Phillips, J. 2009. 'Alfred Chester Beatty: Mining Engineer, Financier, and Entrepreneur, 1898–1950', in R.E. Dumett (ed.), *Mining Tycoons in the Age of Empire, 1870–1945: Entrepreneurship, High Finance, Politics and Territorial Expansion*. Ashgate: Farnham, pp. 215–38.

Pim, A. 1938. *Report of the Commission Appointed to Enquire into the Financial and Economic Position of Northern Rhodesia*. London: His Majesty's Stationery Office.

Piot, C. 1999. *Remotely Global: Village Modernity in West Africa*. Chicago: University of Chicago Press.

Polanyi, K. 2001. *The Great Transformation: The Political and Economic Origins of Our Time*. Boston: Beacon Press.

Porteous, J.D. 1972. 'The Imposed Total Environment: Pattern and Response', *Man-Environment* 2(1): 63–64.

Postel, H. 2017. 'Moving beyond "China in Africa": Insights from Zambian Immigration Data', *Journal of Current Chinese Affairs* 46(2): 155–74.

Potter, J.G. 1971. 'The 51 Per Cent Nationalisation of the Zambian Copper Mines', in M.L.O. Faber and J.G. Potter (eds), *Towards Economic Independence: Papers on the Nationalisation of the Copper Industry in Zambia*. London: Cambridge University Press, pp. 91–134.

Potts, D. 2005. 'Counter-Urbanisation on the Zambian Copperbelt? Interpretations and Implications', *Urban Studies* 42(4): 583–609.

Powdermaker, H. 1962. *Copper Town: Changing Africa*. New York: Harper & Row.

Prain, R.L. 1956. 'The Stabilization of Labour in the Rhodesian Copper Belt', *African Affairs* 55(221): 305–12.

RACM. 1951. 'Reports and Accounts for the Year Ended 30th June, 1951', 30 June, SELECTION TRUST/TEMP/G/55. LSE Library Archives, London.

———. 1957. 'Proposed New African Township: Report on Outline Advisory Development Plan and Detailed Planning of First Portion', April, 21.6.2F. ZCCM-IH Archives, Ndola.

———. 1960a. 'General Notes: The Amenities Which Will Be Required', 11.2.3B. ZCCM-IH Archives, Ndola.

———. 1960b. 'Social Services at Mpatamatu Township (draft)', 11.2.3D. ZCCM-IH Archives, Ndola.

———. 1961a. 'Construction of 323 African Dwellings (317 Buildings) and Essential Services to Same in Precincts no. 3 of Mpatamatu Township: Form of Tender', 14 August, 12.5.5B. ZCCM-IH Archives, Ndola.

———. 1961b. 'Merger with Rhodesian Selection Trust Limited', 14 December, 14.2.7F. ZCCM-IH Archives, Ndola.

———. 1962. 'Notes of a Meeting between Engineering Department and African Personnel Department', 17 August, 10.6.10D. ZCCM-IH Archives, Ndola.

RAID. 2000. *Zambia, Deregulation and the Denial of Human Rights: Submission to the Committee on Economic, Social and Cultural Rights*. Oxford: RAID.

Rajak, Dinah. 2011. *In Good Company: An Anatomy of Corporate Social Responsibility*. Stanford: Stanford University Press.

RAMCOZ (in receivership). 2001. 'Listing of Social/Non Core Assets', 1 October, Document Courtesy of Fackson Mugala, Luanshya.

———. 2004. 'List', Document Courtesy of Fackson Mugala, Luanshya.

———. 2013. 'Properties for Sale', *The Post*, 18 January.

RCM Luanshya Division. 1971. 'Proposed Programme of Expenditure Chargeable to Provision for Replacements for the Year Ending 30th June, 1971: Extension of Mpatamatu Payline', 30 June, 1.1.3B. ZCCM-IH Archives, Ndola.

———. 1972. 'Proposed Programme of Expenditure Chargeable to Capital Account for the Year Ending 30th June, 1972: Housing and Transport', 30 June, 1.1.3B. ZCCM-IH Archives, Ndola.

———. 1974. 'Contract for Houses and Associated Engineering Services at Mpatamatu Precinct 5: Conditions of Contract, Form of Tender, Specification and Bills of Quantities', July, 12.5.7E. ZCCM-IH Archives, Ndola.

———. 1977. 'Youth Development Programmes Luanshya Division', 8 November, 11.2.10C. ZCCM-IH Archives, Ndola.

Reed, I.A. 2011. *Interpretation and Social Knowledge: On the Use of Theory in the Human Sciences*. Chicago: University of Chicago Press.

Republic of Zambia. 1982. 'Certificate of Incorporation', 25 March, 11.6.6E. ZCCM-IH Archives, Ndola.

Rhodian. 1959. 'Copper and the Postage Stamp', *Horizon* (September): 16–17.

Richards, A.I. 1969. *Land, Labour and Diet in Northern Rhodesia: An Economic Study of the Bemba Tribe.* London: Oxford University Press.

RMMTMB. 1970. 'Community Development Report', March, 11.3.5B. ZCCM-IH Archives, Ndola.

———. 1974a. 'Department of Community Development Monthly Report', July, 21.6.2D. ZCCM-IH Archives, Ndola.

———. 1974b. 'Minutes of Ward Council Meeting Held at Buseko Hall', 20 January, 21.6.2D. ZCCM-IH Archives, Ndola.

———. 1975. 'Community Development Department Report', January, 21.6.2D. ZCCM-IH Archives, Ndola.

———. 1977. 'Mpatamatu Ward Development Council', 3 September, 11.2.10C. ZCCM-IH Archives, Ndola.

———. 1978. 'Invitation Christmas Come-Together Party', 22 December, 11.2.10C. ZCCM-IH Archives, Ndola.

Roberts, A.D. 1976. *A History of Zambia.* London: Heinemann.

———. 1982. 'Notes towards a Financial History of Copper Mining in Northern Rhodesia', *Canadian Journal of African Studies* 16(2): 347–59.

Robinson, E.A.G. 1967. 'The Economic Problem', in J.M. Davis (ed.), *Modern Industry and the African.* New York: Augustus M. Kelley, pp. 130–224.

RST Roan Antelope Division. 1962a. 'Engineering Department: Work in Hand for African Personnel Department', June, 10.6.10D. ZCCM-IH Archives, Ndola.

———. 1962b. 'Memorandum: Utilisation of Excess Open Spaces', 16 June, T21.2A. ZCCM-IH Archives, Ndola.

———. 1962c. 'Notes of a Meeting between Engineering Department and African Personnel Department at the Main Office', 17 August, 10.6.10D. ZCCM-IH Archives, Ndola.

———. 1962d. 'Replacement and Obsolescence Reserve Expenditure Year 1962/63 Appropriation Request No. R. 1838: Housing–Mpatamatu Township', 10 April. Office of the Receiver, Luanshya.

———. 1963a. 'Memorandum Roman Catholic Church – Mpatamatu', 17 June, T21.2A. ZCCM-IH Archives, Ndola.

———. 1963b. 'Provision for Replacements Year 1963/64 Appropriation Request No. R.1941: Housing – Mpatamatu Township', 18 March, Office of the Receiver, Luanshya.

———. 1963c. 'Provision for Replacements Year 1963/64 Appropriation Request No. R. 1944: Welfare Centre – Mpatamatu Township', 18 March, Office of the Receiver, Luanshya.

———. 1964a. 'Confidential', 8 April, 16.3.7A. ZCCM-IH Archives, Ndola.

———. 1964b. 'Contract CS19 for the Erection of 200 to 325 Houses and Services thereto in Roan and Mpatamatu Townships', June, 12.5.7E. ZCCM-IH Archives, Ndola.

————. 1964c. 'Contract for 325 Dwelling Units and Essential Services thereto in Precinct no. 4 of Mpatamatu Township and in Makoma and Bwafwano Villages of Roan Township', 5 August, 12.5.7E. ZCCM-IH Archives, Ndola.

————. 1964d. 'Liquor Undertaking in Roan and Mpatamatu Mine Township', 16 April, 16.3.7A. ZCCM-IH Archives, Ndola.

————. 1964e. 'Provisions for Replacement Year 1964/65 Appropriation Request No. R. 2025: New Housing: Roan and Mpatamatu Townships', Office of the Receiver, Luanshya.

————. 1964f. 'High Density Housing Requirements: Roan and Mpatamatu Townships', 3 April, 14.1.7F. ZCCM-IH Archives, Ndola.

————. 1966a. 'Minutes of a Meeting Held between the General Manager and the Club Chairmen, 1966 in the General Office Conference Room', 20 April, 11.6.4B. ZCCM-IH Archives, Ndola.

————. 1966b. 'New Taverns in Roan and Mpatamatu Townships', 18 November, 16.3.7A. ZCCM-IH Archives, Ndola.

————. 1968. 'Annual State of Origin of Local Labour Force', 31 December, 16.3.9A. ZCCM-IH Archives, Ndola.

————. Undated. 'Citizens Handbook', 11.8.5F. ZCCM-IH Archives, Ndola.

Russell, W.A. 1935. *Report of the Commission Appointed to Inquire into the Disturbances in the Copperbelt, Northern Rhodesia*. London: His Majesty's Stationery Office.

SASAC. 2020. '*Yangqi minglu* [Company list]', 5 June. Retrieved 24 September 2020 from http://www.sasac.gov.cn/n2588035/n2641579/n2641645/index.html.

Sautman, B. 2013. 'The Chinese Defilement Case: Racial Profiling in an African "Model of Democracy"', *Rutgers Race and the Law Review* 14(1): 87–134.

Schatz, J.J. 2006. 'Zambian Hopeful Takes a Swing at China', *Washington Post*, 25 September. Retrieved 23 August 2018 from http://www.washingtonpost.com/wp-dyn/content/article/2006/09/24/AR2006092400915.html.

Schlee, G. 2008. *How Enemies Are Made: Towards a Theory of Ethnic and Religious Conflicts*. New York: Berghahn Books.

————. 2018. 'Difference and Sameness as Modes of Integration', in G. Schlee and A. Horstmann (eds), *Difference and Sameness as Modes of Integration: Anthropological Perspectives on Ethnicity and Religion*. New York: Berghahn Books, pp. 1–32.

Schumaker, L. 2001. *Africanizing Anthropology: Fieldwork, Networks, and the Making of Cultural Knowledge in Central Africa*. Durham: Duke University Press.

————. 2008. 'Slimes and Death-Dealing Dambos: Water, Industry and the Garden City on Zambia's Copperbelt', *Journal of Southern African Studies* 34(4): 823–40.

————. 2011. 'The Mosquito Taken at the Beerhall: Malaria Research and Control on Zambia's Copperbelt', in P.W. Geissler and C. Molyneux (eds),

Evidence, Ethos and Experiment: The Anthropology and History of Medical Research in Africa. New York: Berghahn Books, pp. 403–27.

Schwenkel, C. 2013. 'Post/Socialist Affect: Ruination and Reconstruction of the Nation in Urban Vietnam', *Cultural Anthropology* 28(2): 252–77.

Seed Co. 2018. 'Our Story'. Retrieved 29 August 2018 from http://www.seed cogroup.com/about-us/our-story.

Selection Trust. Undated. 'Mr. A. Chester Beatty: The First Selection Trust Limited and Its Entry into the Northern Rhodesian Copper Business', SELECTION TRUST/TEMP/G/44. LSE Library Archives, London.

Shacinda, S. 2009. 'Zambia Picks China Firm to Run Luanshya Copper Mine', *Reuters*, 8 May. Retrieved 22 August 2018 from http://www.reuters.com/ article/minerals-zambia-luanshya-idUSWEB40020090508.

Siegel, B. 1988. 'Bomas, Missions, and Mines: The Making of Centres on the Zambian Copperbelt', *African Studies Review* 31(3): 61–84.

———. 1989. 'The "Wild" and "Lazy" Lamba: Ethnic Stereotypes on the Central African Copperbelt', *Anthropology Publications* 5: 1–16.

———. 2008. 'Water Spirits and Mermaids: The Copperbelt *Chitapo*', *Anthropology Publications* 2: 1–22.

Simmel, G. 1958. 'Two Essays', *The Hudson Review* 11(3): 371–85.

Simutanyi, N. 1996. 'The Politics of Structural Adjustment in Zambia', *Third World Quarterly* 17(4): 825–39.

Sklar, R.L. 1975. *Corporate Power in an African State: The Political Impact of Multinational Mining Companies in Zambia*. Berkeley: University of California Press.

Smart, J. 2014. 'Urban Agriculture and Economic Change in the Zambia Copperbelt: The Cases of Ndola, Kitwe and Luanshya', Ph.D. dissertation. Dunedine: University of Otago.

Smith, H.H. 1985. 'The Territorial and Civic Heraldry of Northern Rhodesia Up to the End of the Federation', *ARMA: Quarterly Bulletin of the Heraldry Society of Southern Africa* 28(109): 1480–94.

South African CSIR. 1947a. 'Minutes of the First Meeting of the Estate Planning Sub-Committee', 7 October, AD1715. Historical Papers Research Archive of the South African Institute of Race Relations, Johannesburg. Retrieved 11 July 2017 from http://www.historicalpapers.wits.ac.za/inventories/inv_ pdfo/AD1715/AD1715-8-5-10-001-jpeg.pdf.

———. 1947b. 'Minutes of the Second Meeting of the Research Committee on Minimum Standards of Accommodation', 4 December, AD1715. Historical Papers Research Archive of the South African Institute of Race Relations, Johannesburg. Retrieved 11 July 2017 from http://www.historicalpapers.wits .ac.za/inventories/inv_pdfo/AD1715/AD1715-8-5-22-001-jpeg.pdf.

———. 1948. 'Research Committee on Minimum Standards of Accommodation: The Joint Advisory Committee on Urban African Housing', 27 May,

AD1715. Historical Papers Research Archive of the South African Institute of Race Relations, Johannesburg. Retrieved 11 July 2017 from http://www .historicalpapers.wits.ac.za/inventories/inv_pdfo/AD1715/AD1715-8-6-16-001-jpeg.pdf.

Sparks, S.J. 2012 'Apartheid Modern: South Africa's Oil from Coal Project and the History of a South African Company Town', Ph.D. dissertation. Ann Arbor: University of Michigan.

Spearpoint, C.F. 1937. 'The African Native and the Rhodesian Copper Mines', *Journal of the Royal African Society* 36(144): 1–56.

———. 1953. 'African Labour Affairs at the Roan Antelope Mine, 1927–1950', in M. Watson (ed.), *African Highway: The Battle for Health in Central Africa*. London: John Murray, pp. 12–16.

Spilker, M. 2010. '800 Jahre Mansfelder Kupferschieferbergbau', *Karstwanderweg Südharz*, 6 March. Retrieved 1 February 2018 from https://www.karst wanderweg.de/sympo/12/spilker/index.htm.

Star, S.L., and K. Ruhleder. 1996. 'Steps Toward an Ecology of Infrastructure: Design and Access for Large Information Spaces', *Information Systems Research* 7(1): 111–34.

Starc, G. 2010. 'Sportsmen of Yugoslavia, Unite: Workers' Sport between Leisure and Work', in B. Luthar and M. Pušnik (eds), *Remembering Utopia: The Culture of Everyday Life in Socialist Yugoslavia*. Washington: New Academia Publishing, pp. 259–88.

Stoler, A.L. 2008a. 'Epistemic Politics: Ontologies of Colonial Common Sense', *The Philosophical Forum* 39: 349–61.

———. 2008b. 'Imperial Debris: Reflections on Ruins and Ruination', *Cultural Anthropology* 23(2): 191–219.

———. 2013. 'Introduction "The Rot Remains": From Ruins to Ruination', in A.L. Stoler (ed.), *Imperial Debris: On Ruins and Ruination*. Durham: Duke University Press, pp. 1–35.

———. 2016. *Duress: Imperial Durabilities in Our Times*. Durham: Duke University Press.

Stoler, A.L., and C. McGranahan. 2007. 'Introduction: Refiguring Imperial Terrains', in A.L. Stoler, C. McGranahan and P.C. Perdue (eds), *Imperial Formations*. Santa Fe: School for Advanced Research Press, pp. 3–42.

Straube, C. 2020. 'Speak, Friend, and Enter? Fieldwork Access and Anthropological Knowledge Production on the Copperbelt', *Journal of Southern African Studies* 46(3): 399–415.

———. 2021. 'Of Corporate Welfare Buildings and Private Initiative: Post-Paternalist Ruination and Renovation in a Former Zambian Mine Township', in M. Larmer, E. Guene, B. Henriet, I. Peša and R. Taylor (eds), *Across the Copperbelt: Urban and Social Change in Central Africa's Borderland Communities*. Oxford: James Currey.

Studdert, D., and V. Walkerdine. 2016. *Rethinking Community Research: Inter-relationality, Communal Being and Commonality*. London: Palgrave Macmillan.

Stürmer, M. 2009. *China und die internationalen Rohstoffmärkte*. Saarbrücken: Vdm Verlag Dr. Müller.

Taylor, J.V., and D.A. Lehmann. 1961. *Christians of the Copperbelt: The Growth of the Church in Northern Rhodesia*. London: SCM.

Tembo, A.K. 2009. 'Conceptualising Quality in Health Care as Perceived and Experienced by Households: A Case Study of Privatising Zambia Consolidated Copper Mines, Luanshya Division', Master's thesis. Johannesburg: University of Witwatersrand.

The Times. 1968. 'Sir Alfred Chester Beatty: Philanthropic Mining Millionaire and Art Collector', 22 January.

Thomson, J. 1893. 'To Lake Bangweulu and the Unexplored Region of British Central Africa', *The Geographical Journal* 1(2): 97–115.

Tregenza, J.M. 1988. 'Reade, Charles Compton (1880–1933)', *Australian Dictionary of Biography*. Retrieved 24 September 2020 from http://adb.anu.edu.au/biography/reade-charles-compton-8166.

Tsing, A.L. 2015. *The Mushroom at the End of the World: On the Possibility of Life in Capitalist Ruins*. Princeton: Princeton University Press.

United Nations Children's Emergency Fund Eastern and Southern Africa. 2017. 'MDGi Hands over Refurbished Copperbelt Health Facilities to Ministry of Health', UNICEF. Retrieved 20 January 2021 from https://www.unicef.org/zambia/press-releases/mdgi-hands-over-four-refurbished-health-centres-ministry-health-lusaka-and.

Unsworth, E.I.G. 1957. *The Laws of Northern Rhodesia*. Lusaka: Government Printer.

Ushewokunze, C.M. 1974. 'The Legal Framework of Copper Production in Zambia', *Zambia Law Journal* 6: 75–100.

Utzinger, J., Y. Tozan, F. Doumani and B.H. Singer. 2002. 'The Economic Payoffs of Integrated Malaria Control in the Zambian Copperbelt between 1930 and 1950', *Tropical Medicine and International Health* 7(8): 657–77.

Victoria, J.L.E. 2016. 'Anthropology of Power: Beyond State-Centric Politics', *Anthropological Theory* 16(2–3): 249–62.

Wangwe, M. 2015. 'Baluba Mine Closes. . . 1,640 Miners' Jobs Put on Hold and Luanshya Mine Shuts Its Treatment Plant', *The Post*, 7 September. Retrieved 16 July 2016 from http://www.postzambia.com/news.php?id=11121.

———. 2016. 'Security Guard in Hospital after Botched Theft of Power Cable', *The Post*, 29 June. Retrieved 8 December 2017 from http://www.postzambia.com/news.php?id=18991.

Waters, H. 2019. 'Undermining the Urban Present: Struggles over Toxicity and Environmental Knowledge in Zambian Mining Cities', Ph.D. dissertation. Minneapolis: University of Minnesota.

Watson, M. 1953. 'A Conquest of Disease', in M. Watson (ed.), *African Highway: The Battle for Health in Central Africa*. London: John Murray, pp. 68–71.

Werbner, R.P. 1984. 'The Manchester School in South-Central Africa', *Annual Review of Anthropology* 13: 157–85.

Whelan, F.J. 1963. *Northern Rhodesia Government: Report of the Commission of Inquiry into Unrest on the Copperbelt, July–August 1963*. Lusaka: Government Printer.

Wilson, G. 1941. 'An Essay on the Economics of Detribalization in Northern Rhodesia, Parts I', *Rhodes-Livingstone Papers 5*.

———. 1942. 'An Essay on the Economics of Detribalization in Northern Rhodesia, Parts II', *Rhodes-Livingstone Papers 6*.

Wilson, J. 2012. 'The Day a Team Died: A Tragedy for Zambian Football', *The Independent*, 19 January. Retrieved 22 February 2017 from http://www.independent.co.uk/sport/football/international/the-day-a-team-died-a-tragedy-for-zambian-football-6291475.html.

World Bank. 2000. 'Mine Township Services Project', *World Bank*, 20 June. Retrieved 18 August 2017 from http://projects.worldbank.org/P064064/mine-township-services-project?lang=en.

Yarrow, T. 2017. 'Remains of the Future: Rethinking the Space and Time of Ruination through the Volta Resettlement Project, Ghana', *Cultural Anthropology* 32(4): 566–91.

Zambia National Heritage Conservation Commission. 1989. 'National Heritage Conservation Commission Act, Cap 173: Collier Monument Roan Antelope Copper Mine', Zambia Legal Information Institute. Retrieved 23 August 2018 from https://zambialii.org/zm/legislation/consolidated_act/173.

ZCCM. 1984. 'Guidelines on ZCCM Sponsored Sports Programmes', 14 March, 12.2.9E. ZCCM-IH Archives, Ndola.

———. 1985. 'Leasing of Mine Taverns', 27 February, 12.8.9F. ZCCM-IH Archives, Ndola.

———. 1991. 'Commissioning of Mpatamatu Sports Complex', 3.4.4E. ZCCM-IH Archives, Ndola.

———. 1992. '1992 ZCCM Youth Cross Country Championship', 10 March, 3.4.4E. ZCCM-IH Archives, Ndola.

Index

abjection. *See under* Ferguson, James

Achebe, Chinua, 1, 115

African National Congress, 71

Agamben, Giorgio. *See* corporate
    paternalism: camps

Baluba mine. *See under* Luanshya

Bayport Financial Services, 43, 45, 47n27

Beatty, Alfred Chester, 22–23, 24. *See also*
    Roan Antelope Copper Mines

Beira, 3, 84

Belgian Congo, 26, 49. *See also* Democratic
    Republic of the Congo

Bemba, 1, 50, 89, 109, 113n1, 113n12

Binani Industries, 41–42, 61, 83. *See also*
    Roan Antelope Mining Corporation
    of Zambia

Blantyre, 19

British Foreign Office, 21

British South Africa Company, 1, 19–21,
    22, 25

Broken Hill. *See* Kabwe

Buna, 9–10, 18nn11–12, 108

Burawoy, Michael
    extended case method, 11, 18n13
    reflexive science, 10–11
    Zambianization, 40, 57
    See also fieldwork: methods

Cape Town, 19, 23

Chanda, Nathan. *See* Luanshya: mayor

chibuku, 87, 90, 99, 113n1. *See also* leisure:
    beer halls

Chile, 99

Chililabombwe, 98

Chiluba, Frederick, 75

China, 112
    anti-Chinese sentiments in Zambia, 5,
        17n4
    China 15th Metallurgical Construction
        Group Corporation, 12, 61
    China Nonferrous Metal Mining
        (Group) Corporation, 4–5
    Chinese studies, 3, 17n1
    CNMC Luanshya Copper Mines, 48,
        117
    investments in Zambia, 4–5, 87, 108,
        111
    migration to Zambia, 5
    Ministry of Commerce, 5, 17n3
    Non-Ferrous China-Africa, 5
    State-owned Assets Supervision and
        Administration Commission of the
        State Council, 5
    Zambia-China Economic and Trade
        Cooperation Zone, 5

Chingola, 7, 107

Chipata, 48, 50
chitenge, 6
Christianity. *See* religion
Chungu, Steven, 6
Cold War, 32
Collier, William, 22–25, 45n3
Collings, J.C., 14, 30, 32–33, 34, 39, 73,
    80, 90, 92, 93, 94
colonialism, 1, 2, 6, 12, 20–26, 27, 29–30,
    33, 36, 39, 46, 49, 50, 54–55, 59, 64,
    88, 95, 100, 116, 117
company town, 17, 33, 38–39, 46, 69, 72,
    73, 83, 84, 99, 116
Copperbelt
    as extractive sphere, 23–26, 100
    Chinese investments (*see* China:
        investments in Zambia)
    foundation of mining towns (*see*
        Luanshya: history)
    geographical location, 7–8, 23
    migration to, 50
    research on, 10–11, 14–15, 21, 51–52,
        71, 99, 111
    strikes (*see* mineworkers: strikes)
copper mining, 6, 8, 14, 17n5, 20, 21,
    22–24, 30–32, 41, 46n5, 63, 87
corporate paternalism
    camps, 27, 38
    concept of, 37–40, 116
    corporate social responsibility, 3, 108,
        117
    gender division, 49–50, 54, 56, 59, 65,
        117–118
    language, 38, 54–55
    life under, 2, 3–4, 9, 11, 12–13, 16, 44,
        75, 88, 92, 99–100, 108, 118, 122
    sports. *See* leisure: sports
    total social institution, 38–39
    unitary structure of the mine, 37–38
    See also nostalgia.
corporate social responsibility. *See under*
    corporate paternalism
Costain, Richard, 34, 46n19
Crawford, Margaret. *See* company town

dambos. *See* Lamba: use of dambos
de Certeau, Michel
    stratified place, 12
    texturology, 53

Democratic Republic of the Congo, 8, 26.
    See also Belgian Congo
dependence. *See under* Ferguson, James
development agreements. *See* Zambia
    Consolidated Copper Mines:
    privatization
Devisch, René. *See* social welfare buildings:
    social engineering, Mususa, Patience:
    villagisation
Diamang, 27

East Germany, 8–9, 108
elections. *See* social welfare buildings: as
    polling stations
Epstein, A.L., 15. *See also* corporate
    paternalism: unitary structure of the
    mine
experience cohorts. *See* fieldwork: research
    participants
extended case method. *See under* Burawoy,
    Michael
extractive community, 27, 39

Ferguson, James
    abjection, 111, 112
    dependence, 40, 66, 98, 108, 112, 122
    Expectations of Modernity, 1, 14, 56
    global disconnect, 111, 112, 121
    on Rhodes-Livingstone Institute, 52,
        66n5 (*see also* Rhodes-Livingstone
        Institute)
fieldwork
    access, 10, 14, 16
    methods, 11–14, 113n12
    politics, 10, 14
    positionality, 14, 108
    research participants, 9, 12–13, 14, 26,
        34, 39, 43, 56, 64, 74, 81, 100, 108,
        118
First Quantum Minerals, 41
football. *See* leisure: sports
Fort Jameson. *See* Chipata
Foucault, Michel
    biopolitics, 37, 57, 96, 100–101
    governmentality, 39, 47n22

Garden City movement, 26, 29–30, 33, 36
Gender, 12, 49, 51, 54, 57, 59, 70, 101,
    116, 117, 119

global disconnect. *See under* Ferguson, James
Gluckman, Max, 52–53, 60. *See also*
    Rhodes-Livingstone Institute
Goffmann, Erving. *See* corporate
    paternalism: total social institution
Gupta, Pamila. *See* renovation.

Harare, 23
Hichilema, Hakainde, 6, 7, 17n7
Horizon. *See* Roan Antelope Copper Mines:
    Horizon company magazine.

imbaula, 43, 56
infrastructure(s)
    concept of, 23–24, 37, 38, 44, 46,
        70–71, 75
    nostalgia for (*see under* nostalgia)
    types of, 7, 33, 36, 41, 42, 49, 50, 65,
        76, 88
    See also social welfare buildings
International Monetary Fund, 40

Japan, 6, 112
Jehovah's Witnesses. *See under* religion
Joshua, Temitope Balogun. *See* religion:
    Synagogue, Church of All Nations

Kabwe, 23, 88
Kafue, 18n8, 19
Kalomo, 23
Kambwili, Chishimba, 6, 82
Kaunda, Francis, 41
Kaunda, Kenneth, 29, 96
Kimberly, 27
Kitwe, 7, 12, 46n14, 54, 55, 73, 98, 101,
    112, 114n51
Konkola Copper Mines, 107
Korean War, 32

Lake Bangweulu, 19
Lake Nyasa, 19
Lake Superior, 57
Lamba
    artisanal mining, 22, 46n2
    Chief Mshiri, 19–21, 22
    language, 18n8
    opposition to mining, 24–26
    snake story, 6, 24–26
    use of dambos, 25, 29

landscaping, 2, 39
Larkin, Brian. *See* infrastructure(s)
leisure
    after school, 12, 61, 98
    beer halls, 88–92, 101, 104
    dancing, 102, 104
    mine clubs, 92–93
    music, 91, 98–99, 103, 106, 107, 120
    structured play, 95
    sports, 96, 98, 100, 101, 104
    stadium, 2, 45, 93–98, 99, 100, 101,
        119, 120
Leopold II., King of Belgium, 24
Lewanika, King of Barotseland, 19
Livingstone, 7, 29
Livingstone, David, 54
Lochner Concession, 19
Luangwa, 19, 20
Luanshya
    as field site, 4–7, 12, 14–15
    Baluba mine, 34, 41, 43, 63, 73, 87, 90
    coat of arms, 6
    history, 6, 15, 19–23, 26–29
    mayor, 91
    Mikomfwa township, 27, 102
    municipal council, 15, 78
    Ndeke township, 68
    Roan township, 7, 12, 30, 36, 53, 54,
        56, 61, 65, 86n21, 89, 90, 91, 93, 98,
        109
    segregation, 26–30, 40, 46, 122
    snake story (*see under* Lamba)
    twin character, 6, 26, 27–28
Luanshya Copper Mines, 42, 63, 96
Luapula, 19, 82
Lungu, Edgar, 6, 7, 18n9
Lusaka, 7, 12, 43, 47n24, 102

malaria, 24–26, 29, 42. *See also* Watson,
    Malcolm
Manchester School. *See* Rhodes-Livingstone
    Institute
Mansfeld, 8
men. *See* mineworkers
Mikomfwa township. *See under* Luanshya
Mindolo township. *See* Kitwe
mineworkers
    families, 11, 12, 36, 50, 54, 55, 61, 63,
        66, 70, 72, 83, 98, 112

health care, 25–26, 27, 33, 37, 45, 61,
    63, 65, 66, 69, 119, 121
housing, 9, 30, 34, 36, 37, 39, 42, 43,
    50–51, 74
labour aristocracy, 61–63, 71–72
stabilization, 49, 52, 53
strikes, 32, 41, 52, 81, 113n5, 113n19
unionism, 15, 32, 37, 52, 92
wages, 55, 61, 67n13, 69, 70, 72
Ministry of Education (Zambia), 23, 69,
    70, 72, 73, 74, 76, 81, 98, 121
Ministry of Health (Zambia), 45, 66, 69,
    119
Mopani Copper Mines, 55, 101
Mozambique, 19, 84
Mpatamatu
    history, 30–36
    name, 7, 18n8
    Nkulumashiba Stream, 52, 80, 86n19,
        98, 118
    schools, 73–74, 80–81, 82
    social welfare buildings (see social welfare
        buildings: in Mpatamatu)
Mpongwe, 7
Mufulira, 98, 104
Mususa, Patience, 15
    trying, 60, 61, 64, 104
    villagisation, 60, 67n12

Nchanga. See Konkola Copper Mines.
Ndeke township. See under Luanshya
Ndola, 7, 12, 14, 15, 22, 29, 78, 86n16,
    98, 113n12
Nkana. See Kitwe.
non-governmental organization, 2, 105,
    119, 121
nostalgia
    concept of, 99–100
    for infrastructure, 85, 99–100, 111, 122
Northern Rhodesia, 20, 22, 29, 30.
nshima, 67.
OpenStreetMap, 13. See also fieldwork:
    methods

Patriotic Front, 6, 73, 103
Pentecostalism. See under religion
power
    concept of, 2, 21, 37, 57, 100–101
    relations of, 11, 14, 18n16, 25, 39, 57

Prain, Ronald, 36
Privatization Negotiation Team. See
    Kaunda, Francis
prosperity gospel. See Pentecostalism

Quelimane, 19

racism, 18n16, 38, 54–55, 57, 59
railways, 23, 121
Rainbow Party, 7, 86n22
Rand (escarpment), 27.
Reade, Charles Compton, 29–30
relations, 11, 13, 16, 21, 38, 39, 40, 52,
    57, 97, 112, 113n3, 115, 116
religion
    Assemblies of God, 104, 110, 111, 119
    Catholic Church, 56, 104, 106, 109
    Churches in a mine township, 33, 37,
        54, 101, 107–108
    Dynamic Worship Church International,
        102, 106
    Hillsong Church, 110
    House of Deliverance, 107, 109
    Jehovah's Witnesses, 24, 106
    Pentecostalism, 106, 107–108, 110–111
    Synagogue, Church of All Nations, 110
    United Church of Zambia, 68, 106
    Watch Tower Movement, 24
renovation
    concept of, 3, 11, 84–85, 119
    in practice, 4, 9, 70, 101, 104, 118–119,
        122
    See also ruination
Rhodes, Cecil, 19, 21
Rhodes-Livingstone Institute, 11, 15,
    51–52, 64, 66n5
Rhokana. See Mopani Copper Mines.
Roan Antelope Copper Mines
    alcohol consumption (see leisure: beer
        halls)
    employment scheme, 50–51, 53, 57, 73
    history, 22, 24–26
    Horizon company magazine, 8, 18n10,
        24, 49
    township construction, 29–30, 32, 33,
        36, 94, 115–116
    See also Beatty, Alfred Chester
Roan Antelope Mining Corporation of
    Zambia, 12, 14, 15, 41–43, 45,

47n26, 61, 63, 65, 76, 78–79, 82, 83, 91, 93, 96, 102, 104, 111, 122
Roan Consolidated Mines, 33, 50, 56, 57, 61, 67n10, 82, 91, 93, 96, 99
Roan Selection Trust, 14, 33, 49, 82, 93
Roan township. *See under* Luanshya
Roberts, Douglas, 34, 46n18
Ross Institute for Tropical Diseases. *See* malaria
ruination
    as broken materiality, 2, 44, 59–60, 76, 80, 83, 90–91, 99–100, 104, 111, 117, 143
    as social experience, 12, 65, 83, 100, 108, 111, 122
    concept of, 2–4, 11, 43–46, 84–85, 116–118, 120–122
    See also renovation
rural-urban dichotomy, 51–53, 64

Salisbury. *See* Harare.
Sata, Michael, 5, 6, 73
Schaerer, V.T., 14, 30, 32–33, 34, 39, 73, 80, 90, 92, 93, 94
Schkopau. *See* Buna
Schumaker, Lyn, 15. *See* fieldwork: politics
Selection Trust. *See* Beatty, Alfred Chester
social change, 40–45, 64–66, 82–85, 106–111
social engineering. *See under* social welfare buildings
social welfare buildings
    as polling stations, 81, 120
    concept of, 2–3, 13, 15, 32–33, 36–39, 72, 83, 100–101, 112, 116, 118, 122
    in Mpatamatu, 36, 45, 92
    privatization of, 41–43, 78
    sitting tenants association, 43
    social engineering, 39
Southern Rhodesia, 27, 50, 59. *See also* Zimbabwe
Spearpoint, Cecil Francis, 25, 26–27, 37–38, 46n9, 89. *See also* Roan Antelope Copper Mines
Stephenson, John Edward 'Chirupula', 25
Stoler, Ann Laura. *See* ruination.
Storke, Arthur, 24. *See also* Roan Antelope Copper Mines

teachers
    health care, 68–69, 75
    housing, 70–71, 74
    strikes, 68, 74
    wages, 65, 72, 74, 81
    See also renovation
Things Fall Apart. *See* Chinua, Achebe
Thomson, Joseph, 19–21. *See also* British South Africa Company
trying. *See under* Mususa, Patience

ubwali. *See* nshima
Union Minière du Haut Katanga, 26, 49
United National Independence Party, 15, 40, 71
United Party for National Development, 6, 7, 86n22
United States of America, 22, 24, 33, 103, 109

van Onselen, Charles. *See* leisure: structured play
villagisation. *See under* Mususa, Patience

Watch Tower Movement. *See under* religion
Watson, Malcolm, 25, 29. *See also* malaria
Windhoek, 27
women
    as dependants in mine townships, 12, 27, 37, 48–51, 55, 57, 58, 63
    as mine employees, 53, 56, 57, 58, 65–66
    domestic maternalism, 58–59 (*see also* corporate paternalism)
    economic activity of, 15, 50, 51, 53, 55, 57, 58, 59, 64–66, 98
    programmes, 53–55, 56–57, 60
    See also mineworkers: families
World Bank, 40, 42, 75, 82

Yeats, William Butler. *See* Achebe, Chinua

Zambezi, 19
Zambia Consolidated Copper Mines.
    privatization, 40–42, 47n23, 116, 119
    social welfare, 42, 57, 61, 74–75
    sports (*see under* leisure)
    wages (*see under* mineworkers)

Zambia Electricity Supply Corporation, 45, 78, 86n15

Zambianization. *See under* Burawoy, Michael

Zimbabwe, 23, 114n29. *See also* Southern Rhodesia

zoning. *See* Luanshya: segregation